ACT®
Math and Science Workbook

ACT®

Math and Science Workbook

By the Staff of Kaplan Test Prep and Admissions

PUBLISHING

New York

© 2009 by Kaplan, Inc.

Published by Kaplan Publishing, a division of Kaplan, Inc.
1 Liberty Plaza, 24th Floor
New York, NY 10006

Printed in the United States of America

10 9 8 7 6 5 4

ISBN-13: 978-1-4277-9770-4

Kaplan Publishing books are available at special quantity discounts to use for sales promotions, employee premiums, or educational purposes. Please email our Special Sales Department to order or for more information at kaplanpublishing@kaplan.com, or write to Kaplan Publishing, 1 Liberty Plaza, 24th Floor, New York, NY 10006.

Table of Contents

Introduction to the ACT

Chapter One: **Understanding the ACT**

Congratulations! By picking up this workbook, you're making a commitment to yourself to learn about the ACT and how you can do your very best on the Science and Math sections of the test. The information in this chapter will tell you what you need to know about how the ACT is written and scored. You'll know what to expect on Test Day, so you can walk into your test center feeling confident and prepared. Going into the ACT with that positive attitude is crucial! Familiarizing yourself with the test structure and working through practice problems are a huge part of creating the mindset that will help you ace the ACT. Let's get started.

ACT STRUCTURE

The ACT is broken down into five sections: English, Math, Reading, Science, and Writing. You can elect to take the ACT with only the first four sections. These sections make up the multiple-choice portion of the ACT. The fifth section, in which you produce an essay, is an optional section.

Predictability

No matter where or when you take the ACT, the order of the sections and the time allotted for each are always the same. This consistency works in your favor: The more you know about what to expect on Test Day, the more confident you'll feel. You may know that one section of the test, let's say, Science, usually seems more challenging for you, but at least you know that Reading will always be section 3. The ACT won't ever surprise you by making the Science section the first thing you see when you open your test booklet. Knowing the structure of the ACT will help you feel in control of your test-taking experience.

The following table summarizes the predictable structure of the ACT:

Section	Time Allotted	Number and Type of Questions
1: English	45 minutes	75 multiple choice
2: Mathematics	60 minutes	60 multiple choice
3: Reading	35 minutes	40 multiple choice
4: Science	35 minutes	40 multiple choice
5: Writing	30 minutes	1 essay prompt

What is a Standardized Test?

Here's your first ACT practice question:

One of the most important ways to succeed on a standardized test is to:

A. Do nothing but practice problems in your spare time the week before the test.
B. Talk to anyone who will listen about how nervous you are.
C. Choose option C for any multiple-choice question you're unsure about.
D. Understand what a standardized test is and why taking it doesn't have to be a demoralizing experience.

Which answer did you choose? Although some of the choices may have made you groan or grimace if you recognized they weren't true, we hope you spotted that option D is the best answer.

As you use this book and apply the Kaplan strategies to work through practice problems, you'll come to see that the test experience need not be demoralizing at all. But how are you feeling now? You may be apprehensive for a variety of reasons. Your own teachers didn't write the test. You've heard the test maker includes trick answers. You feel weak in one of the content areas and don't know how you can possibly improve enough to do well on that test section. Thousands of students will be taking the test.

Let's look carefully at that last reason. The simple fact that thousands of students from different places take the ACT means that the test is necessarily constructed in a deliberate and predictable way. Because it's a standardized test, the ACT must include very specific content and skills that are consistent from one test date to another. The need for standardization, far from making the ACT intimidating, makes it predictable. It's predictable not simply in the layout of the test sections in the booklet, but also in the topics that are tested and even *in the way those topics are tested.* Working the practice problems in this book will help you understand not only how each topic is tested but how to approach the various question types.

If you feel anxious about the predominance of multiple-choice questions on the ACT, think about this fact: For multiple-choice questions, there has to be *only one right answer*, and it's *right there in front of you* in the test booklet. A question that could be interpreted differently by students from different schools, even different parts of the country, who've had different teachers and different high school courses—such a question would never make it onto the ACT. Each question on the ACT is put there to test a specific skill. Either the question or the passage it's associated with (for English, Reading, and Science) *must* include information that allows all students to determine the correct answer.

There can be no ambiguity about which answer is best for a multiple-choice question on a standardized test. This workbook will give you proven Kaplan strategies for finding that answer. The Kaplan strategies, along with your understanding about how the test is structured and written, will put *you* in control of your ACT Test Day experience.

ACT SCORING

Scoring for the Multiple-Choice Sections: Raw Score, Scaled Score, and Percentile Ranking

Let's look at how your ACT composite score is calculated. For each multiple-choice section of the test (English, Mathematics, Reading, and Science), the number of questions you answer correctly is totaled. No points are deducted for wrong answers. The total correct for each section is called the *raw* score for that section. Thus, the highest possible raw score for a section is the total number of questions in that section.

Because each version of the ACT is different (more in the wording of the questions than in the types of questions or skills needed to answer them), a conversion from the raw score to a *scaled* score is necessary. For each version of the ACT that is written, the test maker generates a conversion chart that indicates what scaled score each raw score is equivalent to. The conversion from raw score to scaled score is what allows for accurate comparison of test scores even though there are slight variations in each version of the test. The scaled score ranges from a low of 1 to a high of 36 for each of the four multiple-choice sections. Scaled scores have the same meaning for all different versions of the ACT offered on different test dates.

The score for the first three sections of the ACT is further broken down into subscores, which range from 1 to 18. The subscores for a particular section do *not* necessarily add up to the overall score for the section. The table below lists the subscores that are reported for each section.

Test Section	Subscore Ranges
English (75 questions)	Usage/Mechanics (40 questions)
	Rhetorical Skills (35 questions)
Mathematics (60 questions)	Pre-Algebra/Elementary Algebra (24 questions)
	Intermediate Algebra/Coordinate Geometry (18 questions)
	Plane Geometry/Trigonometry (18 questions)
Reading (40 questions)	Social Studies/Sciences (20 questions)
	Arts/Literature (20 questions)
Science (40 questions)	[no subscores for this section]

What most people think of as the ACT score is the composite score. Your composite score, between 1 and 36, is the average of the four scaled scores on the English, Mathematics, Reading, and Science sections of the test. If, for some reason, you leave any one of these four sections blank, a composite score cannot be calculated.

In addition to the raw score, scaled score, and section subscores, your ACT score report also includes a *percentile ranking*. This is not a score that indicates what percentage of questions you answered correctly on the test. Rather, your percentile ranking provides a comparison between your performance and that of other recent ACT test takers. Your percentile ranking indicates the percentage of ACT test takers who scored the same as or lower than you. In other words, if your percentile ranking is 80, that means that you scored the same as or higher than 80 percent of students.

A raw-to-scaled score conversion chart is necessary to take into account slight variations in the difficulty levels of different versions of the test. In other words, it's not possible to say for every ACT test date that if you answer, for example, 55 out of 75 English questions correctly, your scaled score will always be 24. However, you should know that the variations in each test version—and therefore in the raw-to-scaled score conversion chart—are very slight and should not concern you. The table below gives some *approximate* raw score ranges for each section and the associated scaled score and likely percentile ranking.

	Raw Score and Scale Score Approximate Equivalences				
Scaled Score	English Questions Correct (Total = 75)	Mathematics Questions Correct (Total = 60)	Reading Questions Correct (Total = 40)	Science Questions Correct (Total = 40)	Percentile Ranking
32	70	55–56	34–35	35–36	99
27	61–63	45–47	27–28	30–32	90
24	53–56	36–39	22–25	26–28	75
20	42–46	31–32	18–20	20–21	50

Don't get bogged down in the numbers in this table. We've put it here to help you relax! The big-picture message of the chart is that you can get a good ACT score even if you don't answer every question correctly. In terms of how many questions you need to get right, reaching your ACT score goal is probably not as difficult as you might think.

Scoring for the Writing Section

The ACT essay score ranges from 1 to 12 points, with 12 being the highest. To determine the essay score, two trained graders read your essay and assign it a score between 1 and 6. If, as is usually the case, the two graders' scores do not differ by more than 1 point, then your essay score is the sum of the scores assigned by the two graders. For example, if one grader gives your essay a score of 5 and the other a score of 6, your essay score is 11. In the rare instance that the two graders' scores differ by more than a single point, a third grader reads the essay to resolve the difference.

Because the Writing section of the ACT is optional, not every student takes it, and therefore the Writing score has no effect on the composite score. However, if you opt to take the Writing section of the ACT, you will receive two scores in addition to your composite score. First, you will see your essay score, from 1 to 12. Second, you will see a combined English and Writing score, on a scale of 1 to 36. This score is determined by combining your English section score with your Writing section score. It ranges from 1 to 36. If you opt not to do the Writing section, you will not receive either an essay score or a combined English and Writing score.

ACT REGISTRATION

To get all of the information you need about ACT registration, you should visit the test maker's website, www.actstudent.org. There are two ways to register for the ACT. You can do so online, or you can use a registration packet and send in your forms by mail. If you need a registration packet, you should be able to get one from your school counselor, or you can request one directly via the test maker's website.

Because each testing location can accommodate a limited number of students, you should plan ahead to register for the ACT. In general, the registration deadline is approximately five weeks before the test date. If space is available at a testing location, you are allowed to register after the deadline, but you must pay a late registration fee in addition to the regular test fee.

If you think that registering for the ACT on time is simply a matter of logistics and fees, with no relation to your performance on the test, think again. Individual testing centers have limited space. When you know that you're interested in a particular test date at a particular location, it is worthwhile to register as soon as possible. The earlier you register, the more likely it is that you'll be able to test at your preferred location. Many students prefer to test at their own high schools, in a familiar setting. The morning of Test Day will go much more smoothly if you don't have to worry about directions to get to an unfamiliar location. Planning ahead for ACT registration can help you avoid such unnecessary distractions.

When you register, you should read all the information the test maker provides. Learn specifically about what to bring with you, including forms of ID, pencils, acceptable calculators, and snacks for the breaks. You should also pay attention to what behaviors are and are not acceptable during the test. The more you know ahead of time about what to expect on Test Day, the more relaxed and confident you'll be going into the test. When you put that confidence together with the Kaplan strategies and practice you'll get from this book, you can look forward to higher scores on your ACT!

Chapter Two: **ACT Strategies**

Now that you've got some idea of the kind of adversary you face in the ACT, it's time to start developing strategies for dealing with this adversary. In other words, you've got to start developing your ACT Mindset.

The ACT, as we've just seen, isn't a normal test. A normal test requires that you rely almost exclusively on your memory. On a normal test, you'd see questions like this:

The "golden spike," which joined the Union Pacific and Central Pacific Railroads, was driven in Ogden, Utah, in May 1869. Who was president of the United States at the time?

To answer this question, you have to resort to memory dredging. Either you know the answer is Ulysses S. Grant or else you don't. No matter how hard you think, you'll **never** be able to answer this question if you can't remember your history.

But the ACT doesn't test your long-term memory. The answer to every ACT question can be found in the test. Theoretically, if you read carefully and understand the words and concepts the test uses, you can get almost any ACT question right. Notice the difference between the regular-test question above and the ACT-type question below:

What is the product of n and m^2, where n is an odd number and m is an even number?

A. An odd number
B. A multiple of four
C. A noninteger
D. An irrational number

Aside from the obvious difference (this question has answer choices, while the other one does not), there's another difference: The ACT question mostly tests your ability to understand a situation rather than your ability to passively remember a fact. Nobody expects you to know off the top of your head what the product of an odd number and the square of an even number is. But the ACT test makers do expect you to be able to roll up your sleeves and figure it out (as we'll do below).

THE ACT MINDSET

Most students take the ACT with the same mindset that they use for normal tests. Their brains are on "memory mode." Students often panic and give up because they can't seem to remember enough. **But you don't need to remember a ton of picky little rules for the ACT. Don't give up on an ACT question just because your memory fails.**

On the ACT, if you understand what a question is really asking on the test, you can almost **always** answer it. For instance, take the math problem above. You might have been thrown by the way it was phrased. "How can I solve this problem?" you may have asked yourself. "It doesn't even have numbers in it!"

The key here, as in all ACT questions, is taking control. Take the question (by the throat, if necessary) and wrestle it into a form you can understand. Ask yourself: What's really being asked here? What does it mean when they say something like "the product of n and m2"?

Well, you might start by putting it into words you might use. You might say something like this: "I've got to take one number times another. One of the numbers is odd and the other is an even number squared. Then I've got to see what kind of number I get as an answer." Once you put the question in your own terms like this, it becomes much less intimidating—and much easier to get right. You'll realize that you don't have to do complex algebraic computations with variables. All you have to do is substitute numbers.

So do it! Try picking some easy-to-use numbers. Say that n is 3 (an odd number) and m is 2 (an even number). Then m^2 would be 4, because 2×2 is 4. And $n \times m^2$ would be 3×4, which is 12—a multiple of four, but not odd, not a noninteger, not an irrational number, and not a perfect square. The only answer that can be right, then, is B.

See what we mean about figuring out the answer creatively rather than passively remembering it? True, there are some things you had to remember here—what even and odd numbers are, how variables and exponents work, and maybe what integers and irrational numbers are. But these are very basic concepts. Most of what you're expected to know on the ACT is like that: basic. (By the way, you'll find such concepts gathered together in the very attractive 100 Key Math Concepts for the ACT section at the end of this book.)

Of course, basic doesn't always mean easy. Many ACT questions are built on basic concepts, but are tough nonetheless. The problem above, for instance, is difficult because it requires some thought to figure out what's being asked. This isn't only true in Math. It's the same for every part of the ACT.

The creative, take-control kind of thinking we call the ACT Mindset is something you want to bring to virtually every ACT question you encounter. As we'll see, being in the ACT Mindset means reshaping the test-taking experience so that you are in the driver's seat.

It means:

- Answering questions **if you** want to (by guessing on the impossible questions rather than wasting time on them).
- Answering questions **when you** want to (by skipping tough but "doable" questions and coming back to them after you've gotten all of the easy questions done).

- Answering questions **how you** want to (by using "unofficial" ways of getting correct answers fast).

And that's really what the ACT Mindset boils down to: taking control and being creative. Solving specific problems to get points as quickly and easily as you can.

What follows are the top ten strategies you need to do just that.

TEN STRATEGIES FOR MASTERING THE ACT

1. Do Question Triage

In a hospital emergency room, the triage nurse is the person who evaluates each patient and decides which ones get attention first and which ones should be treated later. You should do the same thing on the ACT.

Practicing triage is one of the most important ways of controlling your test-taking experience. It's a fact that there are some questions on the ACT that most students could **never** answer correctly, no matter how much time or effort they spent on them.

Example

If $\sec^2 x = 4$, which of the following could be $\sin x$?

A. 1.73205

B. 3.14159

C. $\sqrt{3}$

D. $\dfrac{\sqrt{3}}{2}$

E. Cannot be determined from the given information.

Clearly, even if you could manage to come up with an answer to this question, it would take some time (if you insist on doing so, refer to the explanation below). But would it be worth the time? We think not.

This question clearly illustrates our point: Do question triage on the ACT. The first time you look at a question, make a quick decision about how hard and time-consuming it looks. Then decide whether to answer it now or skip it and do it later.

- If the question looks comprehensible and reasonably doable, do it right away.
- If the question looks tough and time-consuming, but ultimately doable, skip it, circle the question number in your test booklet, and come back to it later.
- If the question looks impossible, forget about it. Guess and move on, **never** to return.

This triage method will ensure you spend the time needed to do all the easy questions before getting bogged down with a tough problem. Remember, every question on a subject test is worth the same number of points. You get no extra credit for test machismo.

Answering easier questions first has another benefit: It gives you confidence to answer harder ones later. Doing problems in the order you choose rather than in the order imposed by the test makers gives you control over the test. Most students don't have time to do all of the problems, so you've got to make sure you do all of the ones you can easily score on!

Do You Know Your Trig?

Okay, since you're reading this, it's obvious that you want to know the answer to the trig question we just looked at. The answer is D. Here's how we got it:

$$\sec^2 x = 4 \qquad \text{given}$$

$$\sec x = 2 \text{ or } -2 \qquad \text{square root both sides}$$

$$\cos x = \frac{1}{2} \text{ or } -\frac{1}{2} \qquad \cos x = \frac{1}{\sec x}$$

$$\cos^2 x = \frac{1}{4} \qquad \text{square both side}$$

$$\sin^2 x = 1 - \frac{1}{4} \qquad \sin^2 x + \cos^2 x = 1$$

$$\qquad\qquad\qquad\qquad \sin^2 x = 1 - \cos^2 x$$

$$\sin^2 x = \frac{3}{4}$$

$$\sin x = \sqrt{\frac{3}{4}} \text{ or } -\sqrt{\frac{3}{4}} \qquad \text{square root both sides}$$

$$\sin x = \frac{\sqrt{3}}{2} \text{ or } -\frac{\sqrt{3}}{2} \qquad \sqrt{4} = 2$$

$$\sin x = \frac{\sqrt{3}}{2} \text{ or } -\frac{\sqrt{3}}{2} \qquad \sqrt{4} = 2$$

So answer choice D is correct. But if you got it right, don't congratulate yourself quite yet. How long did it take you to get it right? So long that you could have gotten the answers to two easy questions in the same amount of time?

Develop a Plan of Attack

For the English, Reading, and Science sections, the best plan of attack is to do each passage as a block. Make a longish first pass through the questions (call it the "triage" pass), doing the easy ones, guessing on the impossible ones, and skipping any that look like they might cause trouble. Then, make a second pass (call it the "cleanup pass") and do those questions you think you can solve with some elbow grease.

For Math, you use the same two-pass strategy, except that you move through the whole subject test twice. Work through the doable questions first. Most of these will probably be toward the beginning, but not all. Then come back and attack the questions that look possible but tough or time-consuming.

No matter what subject test you're working on, **you should take pains to grid your answers in the right place.** It's easy to misgrid when you're skipping around, so be careful. And of course: *Make sure you have an answer gridded for every question by the time the subject test is over!*

2. Put the Material into a Form You Can Understand

ACT questions are rarely presented in the simplest, most helpful way. In fact, your main job for many questions is to figure out what the question means so you can solve it.

Since the material is presented in such an intimidating way, one of your best strategies for taking control is to recast (reword) the material into a form you can handle better. This is what we did in the math problem about "the product of n and m^2." We took the question and reworded it in a way we could understand.

Mark Up Your Test Booklet

This strategy should be employed on all four subject tests. For example, in Reading, many students find the passages overwhelming: 85 to 90 lines of dense verbiage for each one! But the secret is to put the passages into a form you can understand and use. Circle or underline the main idea, for one thing. And make yourself a road map of the passage, labeling each paragraph so you understand how it all fits together. That way, you'll also know—later, when you're doing the questions—where in the passage to find certain types of information you need. (We'll show you how to do all of these things in the Skill-Building Workouts.)

Reword the Questions

You'll find that you also need to do some recasting of the *questions*. For instance, take this question from a Science passage.

Example:

Figure 1

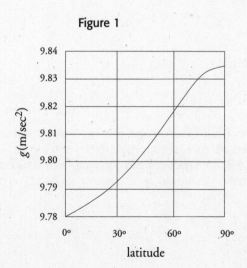

According to Figure 1, at approximately what latitude would calculations using an estimated value at sea level of $g = 9.80$ m/sec^2 produce the least error?

A. 0°
B. 20°
C. 40°
D. 80°

At what latitude would the calculations using a value of $g = 9.80$ m/sec^2 produce the least error? Yikes! What does that mean?

Take a deep breath. Ask yourself: Where would an estimate for g of 9.80 m/sec^2 produce the least error? In a latitude where 9.80 m/sec^2 is the real value of g. If you find the latitude at which the real value of g is 9.80 m/sec^2, then using 9.80 m/sec^2 as an estimate there would produce no error at all!

So, in other words, what this question is asking is: At what latitude does $g = 9.80$ m/sec^2? Now that's a form of the question you can understand. In that form, you can answer it easily: choice C, which you can get just by reading the chart.

Draw Diagrams

Sometimes, putting the material into a usable form involves drawing with your pencil. For instance, take a look at the following math problem.

Example

Jason bought a painting with a frame 1 inch wide. If the dimensions of the outside of the frame are 5 inches by 7 inches, which of the following could be the length of one of the sides of the painting inside the frame?

F. 3 inches

G. 4 inches

H. $5\frac{1}{2}$ inches

J. $6\frac{1}{2}$ inches

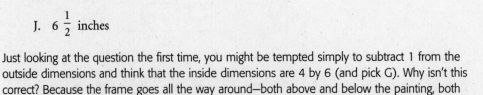

Just looking at the question the first time, you might be tempted simply to subtract 1 from the outside dimensions and think that the inside dimensions are 4 by 6 (and pick G). Why isn't this correct? Because the frame goes all the way around—both above and below the painting, both to the right and to the left. This would have been clear if you had put the problem in a form you could understand and use.

For instance, you might have made the situation graphic by actually sketching out the painting frame (who says you don't have to be an artist to succeed at the ACT?):

When you draw the picture frame like this, you realize that if the outside dimensions are 5 by 7, the inside dimensions must be 3 by 5. Thus, the correct answer is F.

So remember: On the ACT, you've got to put everything into a form that you can understand and use.

3. Ignore Irrelevant Issues

It's easy to waste time on ACT questions by considering irrelevant issues. Just because an issue looks interesting, or just because you're worried about something, doesn't make it important.

Example

. . . China was certainly one of the cradles
of civilization. <u>It's obvious that, China</u>
                          14
<u>has a long history.</u> As is the case with
       14
other ancient cultures, the early history of
China is lost in mythology. . .

14. F. NO CHANGE

   G.   It's obvious that China has a long history.

   H.   Obviously; China has a long history.

   J.   OMIT the underlined portion.

In this question, the test makers are counting on you to waste time worrying about punctuation. Does that comma belong? Can you use a semicolon here? These issues might be worrisome, but there's a bigger issue here—namely, does the sentence belong in the passage at all? No, it doesn't. If China has an ancient culture and was a cradle of civilization, it must have a long history, so the sentence really is "obvious." Redundancy is the relevant issue here, not punctuation. Choice J is correct.

Remember, you've got limited time, so don't get caught up in issues that won't get you a point.

4. Check Back

Remember, the ACT is not a test of your memory, so don't make it one. All of the information you need is in the test itself. Don't be afraid to refer to it. Much of the information is too complex to accurately remember anyway.

In Reading and Science, always refer to the place in the passage where the answer to a question can be found (the question stem will often contain a line reference or a reference to a specific table, graph, or experiment to help you out). Your chosen answer should match the passage—not in exact vocabulary or units of measurement, perhaps, but in meaning.

Example

Isaac Newton was born in 1642 in the hamlet of Woolsthorpe in Lincolnshire, England. But he is more famous as a man of Cambridge, where he studied and taught...

Which of the following does the author imply is a fact about Newton's birth?

A. It occurred in Lincoln, a small hamlet in England.
B. It took place in a part of England known for raising sheep.
C. It did not occur in a large metropolitan setting.
D. It caused Newton to seek his education at Cambridge.

You might expect the right answer to be that Newton was born in a hamlet, or in Woolsthorpe, or in Lincolnshire. But none of those is offered as a choice. Choice A is tempting, but wrong. Newton was born in Lincolnshire, not Lincoln. Choice B is actually true, but it's wrong here. As its name suggests, Woolsthorpe was once known for its wool—which comes from sheep. But the question asks for something implied in the passage.

The correct answer here is C, because a hamlet is a small village. That's not a large metropolitan setting. (It's also a famous play, but that's not among the choices.)

Checking back is especially important in Reading and Science, because the passages leave many people feeling adrift in a sea of details. Often, the wrong answers will be "misplaced details"—details taken from different parts of the passage. They are things that don't answer the question properly but that might sound good to you if you aren't careful. By checking back with the passage, you can avoid choosing such devilishly clever wrong choices.

There's another important lesson here: **Don't pick a choice just because it contains key words you remember from the passage.** Many wrong choices, like D in the question above, are distortions—they use the right words but say the wrong things about them. Look for answer choices that contain the same ideas you find in the passage.

One of the best ways to avoid choosing misplaced details and distortions is to check back with the passage.

5. Answer the Right Question

This strategy is a natural extension of the last. As we said, **the ACT test makers often include among the wrong choices for a question the correct answer to a different question.** Under time pressure, it's easy to fall for one of these red herrings, thinking that you know what's being asked for when really you don't.

Example

What is the value of $3x$ if $9x = 5y + 2$ and $y + 4 = 2y - 10$?

A. 5

B. 8

C. 14

D. 24

To solve this problem, we need to find y first, even though the question asks about x (because x here is given only in terms of y). You could solve the second equation like this:

$y + 4 = 2y - 10$	given
$4 = y - 10$	by subtracting y from both sides
$14 = y$	by adding 10 to both sides

But choice C, 14, isn't the right answer here, because the question doesn't ask for the value of y—it asks about x. We can use the value of y to find x, however, by plugging the calculated value of y into the first equation:

$9x = 5y + 2$	given
$9x = 5(14) + 2$	because $y = 14$
$9x = 70 + 2$	
$9x = 72$	

But E, 72, isn't the answer either, because the question doesn't ask for 9x. It doesn't ask for x either, so if you picked B, 8, you'd be wrong as well. Remember to refer to the question! The question asks for 3x. So we need to divide 9x by 3:

$9x = 72$	from above
$3x = 24$	dividing by 3

Thus, the answer is D.

Always check the question again before choosing your answer. Doing all the right work but then getting the wrong answer can be seriously depressing. So make sure you're answering the right question.

6. Look for the Hidden Answer

On many ACT questions, the right answer is hidden in one way or another. An answer can be hidden by being written in a way that you aren't likely to expect. For example, you might work out a problem and get .5 as your answer, but then find that .5 isn't among the answer choices. Then you notice that one choice reads " $\frac{1}{2}$." Congratulations, Sherlock. You've found the hidden answer.

There's another way the ACT can hide answers. **Many ACT questions have more than one possible right solution, though only one correct answer choice is given. The ACT will hide that answer by offering one of the less obvious possible answers to a question. For example:**

Example

If $3x^2 + 5 = 17$, which of the following could be the value of x?

- A. −3
- B. −2
- C. 0
- D. 1

You quickly solve this very straightforward problem like so:

$3x^2 + 5 = 17$ given

$3x^2 = 12$ by subtracting 5

$x^2 = 4$ dividing by 3

$x = 2$ taking square root of both sides

Having gotten an answer, you confidently look for it among the choices. But 2 isn't a choice. The explanation? This question has two possible solutions, not just one. The square root of 4 can be either 2 or −2. B is thus the answer.

Keep in mind that though there's only one right answer choice for each question, that right answer may not be the one that occurs to you first. A common mistake is to pick an answer that seems "sort of" like the answer you're looking for even when you know it's wrong. Don't settle for second best. If you don't find your answer, don't assume that you're wrong. Try to think of another right way to answer the question.

7. Guess Intelligently

An unanswered question is always wrong, but even a wild guess may be right. On the ACT, a guess can't hurt you, but it can help. In fact, smart guessing can make a big difference in your score. **Always** guess on every ACT question you can't answer. **Never** leave a question blank.

You'll be doing two different kinds of guessing during your two sweeps through any subject test:

- Blind guessing (which you do mostly on questions you deem too hard or time-consuming even to try).
- Considered guessing (which you do mostly on questions that you do some work on, but can't make headway with).

When you guess blindly, you just choose any letter you feel like choosing (Many students like to choose B for Bart; few choose H for Homer). When you guess in a considered way, on the other hand, you've usually done enough work on a question to eliminate at least one or two choices. If you can eliminate any choices, you'll up the odds that you'll guess correctly.

Here are some fun facts about guessing: If you were to work on only half of the questions on the ACT but get them all right, then guess blindly on the other half of the questions, you would probably earn a composite ACT score of around 23 (assuming you had a statistically reasonable success rate on your guesses). A 23 would put you in roughly the top quarter of all those who take the ACT. It's a good score. And all you had to do was answer half the questions correctly.

On the other hand, if you were to hurry and finish all the questions, but get only half of them right, you'd probably earn only a 19, which is below average.

How? Why are you better off answering half and getting them all right instead of answering all and getting only half right?

Here's the trick. The student who answers half the questions right and skips the others can still take guesses on the unanswered questions—and odds are this student will have enough correct guesses to move up 4 points, from a 19 to a 23. But the student who answers all the questions and gets half wrong doesn't have the luxury of taking guesses.

In short: **Guess if you can't figure out an answer for any question!**

8. Be Careful with the Answer Grid

Your ACT score is based on the answers you select on your answer grid. Even if you work out every question correctly, you'll get a low score if you misgrid your answers. So be careful! Don't disdain the process of filling in those little "bubbles" on the grid. Sure, it's mindless, but under time pressure it's easy to lose control and make mistakes.

It's important to **develop a disciplined strategy for filling in the answer grid.** We find that it's smart to grid the answers in groups rather than one question at a time. What this means is this: As you figure out each question in the test booklet, circle the answer choice you come up with. Then transfer those answers to the answer grid in groups of five or more (until you get close to the end of the section, when you start gridding answers one by one).

Gridding in groups like this cuts down on errors because you can focus on this one task and do it right. It also saves time you'd otherwise spend moving papers around, finding your place, and redirecting your mind. Answering ACT questions takes deep, hard thinking. Filling out answer grids is easy, but you have to be careful, especially if you do a lot of skipping around. Shifting between "hard thinking" and "careful bookkeeping" takes time and effort.

In English, Reading, and Science, the test is divided naturally into groups of questions—the passages. For most students, it makes sense to circle your answers in your test booklet as you work them out. Then, when you're finished with each passage and its questions, grid the answers as a group.

In Math, the strategy has to be different because the Math test isn't broken up into natural groups. Mark your answers in the test booklet and then grid them when you reach the end of each page or two. Since there are usually about five math questions per page, you'll probably be gridding five or ten math answers at a time.

No matter what subject test you're working on, though, if you're near the end of a subject test, start gridding your answers one at a time. You don't want to be caught with ungridded answers when time is called.

During the test, the proctor should warn you when you have about five minutes left on each subject test. But don't depend on proctors! Yes, they're usually nice people, but they can mess up once in a while. **Rely on your own watch.** When there's five minutes left in a subject test, start gridding your answers one by one. With a minute or two left, start filling in everything you've left blank. Remember: Even one question left blank could cut your score.

9. Use the Letters of the Choices to Stay on Track

One oddity about the ACT is that even-numbered questions have F, G, H, J (and, in Math, K) as answer choices, rather than A, B, C, D (and, again, E in Math). This might be confusing at first, but you can make it work for you. **A common mistake with the answer grid is to accidentally enter an answer one row up or down. On the ACT, that won't happen if you pay attention to the letter in the answer.** If you're looking for an A and you see only F, G, H, J, and K, you'll know you're in the wrong row on the answer grid.

Another advantage of having answers F through K for even-numbered questions is that it makes you less nervous about patterns in the answers. It's common to start worrying if you've picked the same letter twice or three times in a row. Since the questions have different letters, this can't happen on the ACT. Of course, you could pick the first choice (A or F) for several questions in a row. This shouldn't worry you. It's common for the answers in the same position to be correct three times in a row, and even four times in a row isn't unheard of.

10. Keep Track of Time

During each subject test, you really have to pace yourself. On average, English, Reading, and Science questions should take about 30 seconds each. Math questions should average less than one minute each. Remember to take into account the fact that you'll probably be taking two passes through the questions.

Set your watch to 12:00 at the beginning of each subject test, so it will be easy to check your time. Again, don't rely on proctors, even if they promise that they will dutifully call out the time every 15 minutes. Proctors get distracted once in a while.

For English, Reading, and Science questions, it's useful to check your timing as you grid the answers for each passage. English and Reading passages should take about nine minutes each. Science passages should average about five minutes.

More basic questions should take less time, and harder ones will probably take more. In Math, for instance, you need to go much faster than one per minute during your first sweep. But at the end, you may spend two or three minutes on each of the harder problems you work out.

Take Control

You are the master of the test-taking experience. A common thread in all ten strategies above is: Take control. That's Kaplan's ACT Mindset. Do the questions in the order you want and in the way you want. Don't get bogged down or agonize. Remember, you don't earn points for suffering, but you do earn points for moving on to the next question and getting it right.

BASIC STRATEGY REFERENCE SHEET

The Three Commandments
1. Thou Shalt Learn the Test
- Learn the directions before test day.
- Become familiar with all the subject tests.
- Get a sense of the range of difficulty of the questions.

2. Thou Shalt Learn the Strategies
- Develop a plan of attack for each subject test.
- Develop a guessing strategy that works for you.
- Find "unofficial" ways of finding answers fast.

3. Thou Shalt Learn the Material
- Bone up on weak areas.
- Find out what is and isn't part of the ACT knowledge base.
- Use the ACT Resources section to review important Math and English concepts.

The Top Ten Strategies
1. Do question triage.
2. Put the material into a form you can understand and use.
3. Ignore irrelevant issues.
4. Check back.
5. Answer the right question.
6. Look for the hidden answer.
7. Guess intelligently.
8. Be careful with the answer grid.
9. Use the letters of the choices to stay on track.
10. Keep track of time.

ACT Math

Chapter Three: **Introduction to ACT Math**

TEST BASICS

The ACT Math Test is the second section of the ACT. It is a 60-question, 60-minute test. (Here's some basic math: 60 questions/60 minutes = 1minute per question!) It is completely multiple choice in format and each question is usually discrete (this means no groups of questions referring to the same diagram, picture, etc.). One key way in which the Math Test differs from the other sections is the number of answer choices. The Math Test has five answer choices, while each other section has only four. This means that you will have an additional choice to consider for each question.

Even though all the answers are in multiple-choice form, there are still some differences in the presentation of the questions that you should be prepared to deal with. The main one is that some problems will be basic math problems while others will be word problems. The two problems test the same concepts, but the word problems will require more thought. They simply add another step, since you will have to turn the word problems into a basic math format. Look below for an example.

> **Example:** If a sweater that originally costs $40 is on sale for 15% off, what is the total discount given?
>
> A. $3.00
> B. $4.00
> C. $5.00
> D. $6.00

You need to turn these words into an equation. Ask yourself, what is this problem really asking? It wants you to find 15% of $40. So the equation that you should create is $40 × .15 = $6.00. This means that you are given a discount of $6.00. The answer is D.

Content

The ACT Math test covers material that you are typically expected to have learned up through the end of your junior year. This means that it covers pre-algebra, elementary algebra, intermediate algebra, plane geometry, coordinate geometry, and trigonometry. The relative number of questions on these topics does not change very much from year to year. There are usually about 14 pre-algebra questions, 10 elementary algebra questions, 9 questions each covering intermediate algebra and plane geometry, 14 questions covering plane geometry, and 4 questions covering trigonometry. This may vary by a question or two from year to year, but overall it is relatively unchanged. You are expected to know the basic formulas that are central to each of these content areas as well as be able to discern when to use specific formulas.

Scoring

ACT Math Test scaled scores range from 1 to 36. Along with your overall Math score, you will receive three subscores: a pre-algebra/elementary algebra subscore, an intermediate algebra/coordinate geometry subscore, and a plane geometry/trigonometry subscore. One thing that is important to note about the ACT scoring system is that **THERE IS NO PENALTY FOR WRONG ANSWERS.** This is very important because it means that wrong answers cannot hurt your score. This also means that you should always **ANSWER EVERY QUESTION!**

TIPS FOR THE ACT MATH TEST

Sometimes the textbook approach will be the best way to find the answer. Other times, however, applying common sense or a strategy will get you to the correct answer more quickly and easily. The key is to be open to creative approaches to problem solving. This usually involves taking advantage of the multiple-choice format of the question.

Two methods in particular are extremely useful when you don't see—or would rather not use—the textbook approach to solving a question. These strategies aren't always quicker than more traditional methods, but they're a great way to make confusing problems more concrete. If you can apply these strategies, you're guaranteed to nail that correct answer every time you use them. Let's examine these strategies now.

Picking Numbers

Picking numbers is an extremely handy strategy for making sense of "abstract" problems—ones that insist on dealing with variables rather than numbers. Picking numbers makes abstract problems concrete. On Word Problems, the most common situation where picking numbers comes in handy is when there are variables in the question and in the answer choices. Here's how to apply the method on this type of Word Problem.

Step 1. Pick simple numbers to stand in for the variables.

Step 2. Answer the question using the numbers you picked.

Step 3. Try out all the answer choices using the numbers you picked, eliminating those that gave you a different result.

Step 4. If more than one choice remains, pick a different set of numbers and repeat steps 1–3.

Let's try this strategy on the following problem.

A. $\dfrac{c}{pd}$

B. $\dfrac{pd}{c}$

C. $pd + c$

D. $\dfrac{dc}{p}$

E. $(p - c)d$

If the mere thought of this problem gives you a headache, picking numbers can provide you with a safe way to quickly get to the answer. The key is to pick numbers that make the math easy for you. Since the money will be divided evenly among the charities, pick a number that is a factor of the total amount of money donated ($p \times d$) to make the math go smoothly. Try 2 for p, 8 for d, and 4 for c. Now the question asks: If 2 people each donated 8 dollars to a trust fund that will distribute the money equally among 4 charities, how much money, in dollars, did each charity receive? The answer to this question would be 4 dollars, so replace p with 2, d with 8, and c with 4 in each of the answer choices and see which one comes out to 4.

A. $\dfrac{c}{pd} = \dfrac{4}{2 \times 8} = \dfrac{4}{16} = \dfrac{1}{4}$, which is way too small.

B. $\dfrac{pd}{c} = \dfrac{2 \times 8}{4} = \dfrac{16}{4} = 4$. That's the ticket!

C. $pd + c = 2 \times 8 + 4 = 16 + 4 = 20$. That's too big.

D. $\dfrac{dc}{p} = \dfrac{8 \times 4}{2} = \dfrac{32}{2} = 16$. That's too big.

E. $(p - c)d = (2 - 4) \times 8 = (-2) \times 8 = -16$. That won't work.

Only B works so it must be correct.

Backsolving

Sometimes, a problem will be extremely confusing but the situation won't allow you to pick numbers. When a question has numbers in the choices, refers to an unknown value in the question, or is confusing, but asks a straightforward question, you are probably best off trying to *backsolve* from the choices. When you backsolve, you simply plug the choices back into the question until you find the one that works. If you do this systematically, it shouldn't take much time. Here's the system:

Step 1. Start with B or D.

By starting with **B** or **D** first, you have a 40 percent chance of getting the correct answer in one try.

Step 2. Eliminate choices you know are too big or too small.

The first choice you test is either too small, too large, or correct. Since choices are listed in size order, if you started with **B** and it's too large, **A** would be correct. Likewise, if you started with **D** and it's too small, **E** would be correct.

Step 3. Test the choice that you did *not* start with.

Step 3 is only necessary if you haven't found the answer yet.

If **B** is too small or **D** is too large, you'll have three choices left. In either case, testing the middle remaining choice will immediately reveal the correct answer. For example, if you started with B and it was too small, you would be left with **C, D,** and **E.** If **D** turns out to be too small, **C** would be correct. If it's too large, **E** would be correct.

By predicting if the answer might run small or large (to help you decide whether to start with **B** or **D**) and following this system, you won't have to test more than two of the five choices. In fact, you'll usually only have to test one. Let's try out this strategy on the following problem:

> Thirty people paid a total of $330 for admission to a concert. If each adult paid $15 and each child paid $5, how many adults were admitted to the concert?
>
> A. 15
> B. 18
> C. 20
> D. 22
> E. 24

If algebra isn't your hobby, this problem can be a bit difficult to set up. The question, however, is clear: "How many adults were admitted to the concert?" There's no way to pick numbers here but the numbers in the answer choices suggest that this is an excellent opportunity to backsolve. Adult tickets seem expensive compared to children's tickets, so let's start with **B**.

If 18 adults each paid $15 for admission, the adults would've paid a total of $15 \times 18 = $270. This leaves $330 - $270 = $60 for 30 - 18 = 12 children. $5 \times 12 *does* equal $60. Bingo! That works, so **B** is correct.

Had you started with **D** instead, 22 adults would pay $15 \times 22 = $330. That leaves nothing for 30 - 22 = 8 children, so **D** is too large.

There are three exceptions to following the above order for testing choices:

1. If B or D results in a complex calculation
2. If some of the other answer choices are extremely easy to test
3. If the question asks for the smallest or largest possible value

If plugging in B or D results in an ugly calculation (i.e., if it results in a number that doesn't divide evenly and there are other answer choices that *would* divide evenly), test an easier answer choice instead.

If you're lucky enough to get answer choices with extremely easy numbers to test, such as 0 or 1, test them first since you can evaluate them much faster than most other numbers.

And if the question asks for the smallest or largest possible value of something, you'll want to test the smallest or largest value in the answer choices first.

Remember that on the ACT, all questions are worth the same amount of points regardless of difficulty. If you are stuck on a question, DO NOT spend five minutes trying to get the answer. Instead, move on and answer all the questions you can and come back to that question during a second pass through the test. This will ensure that you answer the most questions correctly. If you are reaching the end of the test and are running out of time, make an educated guess for questions you still have not answered. No matter what, you always want to make sure you have an answer for every single question.

Another strategy that will help you on the ACT is to use your calculator only when necessary. Calculators do not have brains and they will not tell you when you accidentally press 8 even though you mean to press 7. This is a mistake that you can catch yourself if you are writing your notes out on your test booklet. Just about all of the questions on the Math Test can be solved without the use of a calculator and using one too much can actually slow you down on the test. If you are going to bring a calculator to the test, be sure it is one you are familiar with and make sure you have extra batteries.

Special note about calculators: Not all calculators are allowed in the ACT Math Test. Before Test Day, check to make sure your calculator is allowed.

With the 60-minute time limit, many students feel the need to rush through the test because they fear they will run out of time at the end. Time is a factor, but you must still be sure to read each question thoroughly and make sure you understand what it is asking you. For example, a question might ask you to find the circumference of a circle, but gives you the diameter. If you are moving too quickly you might use the diameter in your calculations, even though the formula calls for the use of the radius. The answer you get might even be one of the answer choices because the test makers are aware of the common mistakes that students make. However, by reading thoroughly and working carefully you can avoid mistakes like this. Finally, if you have time at the end of the test, go back and check your work. If there are any questions you are not sure about, double check your calculations.

Now that you are familiar with the structure and scoring of the ACT Math Test, let's move on to review the major content of the test.

Chapter Four: **ACT Math Basics**

The ACT Math Test will cover six main content areas:

Content Area	Number of Questions
Pre-Algebra	14
Elementary Algebra	10
Intermediate Algebra	9
Coordinate Geometry	9
Plane Geometry	14
Trigonometry	4

As you can see, the majority of the test covers algebra concepts. As you review the content below, keep in mind the relative number of questions that are asked on each topic and plan your studying accordingly.

PRE-ALGEBRA

Pre-Algebra questions will test your ability to work with numbers. The following are the basic concepts that you will need to know for the ACT.

Order of Operations

PEMDAS = **P**lease **E**xcuse **M**y **D**ear **A**unt **S**ally: This mnemonic will help you remember the order of operations.

P = Parentheses

E = Exponents

M = Multiplication
D = Division
} in order from left to right

A = Addition
S = Subtraction
} in order from left to right

Example: $30 - 5 \times 4 + (7 - 3)^2 \div 8$

First, perform any operations within **Parentheses.** $30 - 5 \times 4 + 4^2 \div 8$
(If the expression has parentheses within parentheses,
work from the innermost out.)

Next, raise to any powers indicated by **Exponents.** $30 - 5 \times 4 + 16 \div 8$

Then, do all **Multiplication** and **Division** from left to right. $30 - 20 + 2$

Finally, do all **Addition** and **Subtraction** from left to right. $10 + 2 = 12$

Laws of Operations

Commutative law: Addition and multiplication are both **commutative**; it doesn't matter **in what order** the operation is performed.

Example: $5 + 8 = 8 + 5$ $2 \times 6 = 6 \times 2$

Division and subtraction are **not** commutative.

Example: $3 - 2 \neq 2 - 3$ $6 \div 2 \neq 2 \div 6$

Associative law: Addition and multiplication are also **associative**; the terms can be **regrouped** without changing the result.

Example:

$$(a + b) + c = a + (b + c) \qquad (a \times b) \times c = a \times (b \times c)$$
$$(3 + 5) + 8 = 3 + (5 + 8) \qquad (4 \times 5) \times 6 = 4 \times (5 \times 6)$$
$$8 + 8 = 3 + 13 \qquad\qquad 20 \times 6 = 4 \times 30$$
$$16 = 16 \qquad\qquad\qquad 120 = 120$$

Distributive law: The **distributive law** of multiplication allows us to "distribute" a factor among the terms being added or subtracted.

Example:

$$a(b + c) = ab + ac$$
$$4(3 + 7) = 4 \times 3 + 4 \times 7$$
$$4 \times 10 = 12 + 28$$
$$40 = 40$$

Division can be distributed in a similar way.

Example:

$$\frac{3+5}{2} = \frac{3}{2} + \frac{5}{2}$$

$$\frac{8}{2} = 1\frac{1}{2} + 2\frac{1}{2}$$

$$4 = 4$$

Don't get carried away, though. When the sum or difference is in the **denominator**, no distribution is possible.

Example: $\frac{9}{4+5}$ is NOT equal to $\frac{9}{4} + \frac{9}{5}$.

Fractions

$4 \leftarrow$ numerator
$- \leftarrow$ fraction bar (means "divided by")
$5 \leftarrow$ denominator

Equivalent fractions: The value of a number is unchanged if you multiply the number by 1. In a fraction, multiplying the numerator and denominator by the same nonzero number is the same as multiplying the fraction by 1: The fraction is unchanged. Similarly, dividing the top and bottom by the same nonzero number leaves the fraction unchanged.

Example: $\frac{1}{2} = \frac{1 \times 2}{2 \times 2} = \frac{2}{4}$

$$\frac{5}{10} = \frac{5 \div 5}{10 \div 5} = \frac{1}{2}$$

Canceling and reducing: Generally speaking, when you work with fractions on the ACT, you'll need to put them in **lowest terms**. This means the numerator and the denominator are not divisible by any common integer greater than 1. The fraction $\frac{1}{2}$ is in lowest terms, but the fraction $\frac{3}{6}$ is not, since 3 and 6 are both divisible by 3. The method we use to take such a fraction and put it in lowest terms is called **reducing**. That simply means to divide out any common multiples from both the numerator and denominator. This process is also commonly called **canceling.**

Example: Reduce $\frac{15}{35}$ to lowest terms.

First, determine the largest common factor of the numerator and denominator. Then, divide the top and bottom by that number to reduce.

$$\frac{15}{35} = \frac{3 \times 5}{7 \times 5} = \frac{3 \times 5 \div 5}{7 \times 5 \div 5} = \frac{3}{7}$$

KAPLAN)

Addition and subtraction: We can't add or subtract two fractions directly unless they have the same denominator. Therefore, before adding (or subtracting), we must find a common denominator. A common denominator is just a **common multiple** of all the denominators of the fractions. The **least common denominator** is the **least common multiple** (the smallest positive number that is a multiple of all the terms).

Example: $\dfrac{3}{5} + \dfrac{2}{3} - \dfrac{1}{2}$. Denominators are 5, 3, 2.   LCM = $5 \times 3 \times 2 = 30$ = LCD

Multiply the numerator and denominator of each fraction by the value that raises its respective denominator to the LCD. $\left(\dfrac{3}{5} \times \dfrac{6}{6}\right) + \left(\dfrac{2}{3} \times \dfrac{10}{10}\right) - \left(\dfrac{1}{2} \times \dfrac{15}{15}\right)$

$$= \dfrac{18}{16} + \dfrac{20}{30} - \dfrac{15}{30}$$

Combine the numerators by adding or subtracting and keep the LCD as the denominator. $= \dfrac{18+20-5}{30} + \dfrac{23}{30}$

Multiplication:

Example: $\dfrac{10}{9} \times \dfrac{3}{4} \times \dfrac{8}{15}$

First, reduce (cancel) diagonally and vertically. $\dfrac{{}^2\cancel{10}}{{}_3\cancel{9}} \times \dfrac{{}^1\cancel{3}}{{}_1\cancel{4}} \times \dfrac{\cancel{8}^2}{\cancel{15}_3}$

Then, multiply numerators and denominators. $\dfrac{2 \times 1 \times 2}{3 \times 1 \times 3} = \dfrac{4}{9}$

Division: Dividing is the same as multiplying by the **reciprocal** of the divisor. To get the reciprocal of a fraction, invert it by interchanging the numerator and the denominator. The reciprocal of the fraction $\dfrac{3}{7}$ is $\dfrac{7}{3}$.

Example: $\dfrac{4}{3} \div \dfrac{4}{9}$

To divide, invert the second term (the divisor), and then multiply as above.

$$\dfrac{4}{3} \div \dfrac{4}{9} = \dfrac{4}{3} \times \dfrac{9}{4} = \dfrac{{}^1\cancel{4}}{{}_1\cancel{3}} \times \dfrac{\cancel{9}^3}{\cancel{4}_1} = \dfrac{1 \times 3}{1 \times 1} = 3$$

Percents

Percents are one of the most commonly used mathematical relationships and are quite popular on the ACT. *Percent* is just another word for *hundredth*. For example, 27% (27 percent) means:

27 hundredths

$\dfrac{27}{100}$

0.27

27 out of every 100 things

27 parts out of a whole of 100 parts

Making and Dropping Percents

To make a percent, multiply by 100%. Since 100% means 100 hundredths or 1, multiplying by 100% will not change the value.

Example: $0.17 = 0.17 \times 100\% = 17.0\%$ or 17%

Example: $\dfrac{1}{4} = \dfrac{1}{4} \times 100\% = 25\%$

To drop a percent, divide by 100%. Dividing by 100% will not change the value either.

Example: $32\% = \dfrac{32\%}{100\%} = \dfrac{32}{100} = \dfrac{8}{25}$

Example: $\dfrac{1}{2}\% = \dfrac{\frac{1}{2}\%}{100\%} = \dfrac{1}{200}$

Ratios

A ratio is a comparison of two quantities by division.

Ratios may be written with a fraction bar $\left(\dfrac{x}{y}\right)$, with a colon ($x$:$y$), or in English terms (ratio of x to y). We recommend the first way, since ratios can be treated as fractions for the purposes of computation.

Ratios can (and in most cases, should) be reduced to lowest terms just as fractions are reduced.

Example: Max has 16 books and Marie has 12 books.

The ratio of Max's books to Marie's books is $\dfrac{16}{12}$. (Read "16 to 12.")

$\dfrac{16}{12} = \dfrac{4}{3}$ or 4:3

In a ratio of two numbers, the numerator is often associated with the word *of*, and the denominator with the word *to*.

Example: The ratio **of** 3 **to** 4 is $\dfrac{of\ 3}{to\ 4} = \dfrac{3}{4}$.

We frequently deal with ratios by working with a **proportion**. A proportion is simply an equation in which two ratios are set equal to each other.

Rates

A rate is a ratio that relates two different kinds of quantities. Speed (the ratio of distance traveled to time elapsed) is one such example.

When we talk about rates, we usually use the word *per,* as in "miles per hour," "cost per item," and so forth. Since *per* means "for one" or "for each," we express rates as ratios reduced to a denominator of 1.

Example: John travels 50 miles in two hours. His average rate is

$$\frac{50 \text{ miles}}{2 \text{ hours}} = 25 \text{ miles per hour}$$

Note: We frequently speak in terms of "average rate," since it may be improbable (as in the case of speed) that the rate has been constant over the period in question.

Mean, Median, Mode

Mean

The arithmetic **mean**, or **average**, of a group of numbers is defined as the sum of the terms divided by the number of terms.

$$\text{Average} = \frac{\text{Sum of Terms}}{\text{Number of Terms}}$$

Example: Henry buys three items costing $2.00, $0.75, and $0.25. What is the average price?

$$\text{Average price} = \frac{\text{Sum of prices}}{\text{Number of prices}}$$

$$= \frac{\$2.00 + \$0.75 + \$0.25}{3}$$

$$= \frac{\$3.00}{3}$$

$$= \$1.00$$

If we know the average of a group of values and the number of values in the group, we can find the **sum** of the values with the following formula:

$$\text{Sum of Values} = \text{Average Value} \times \text{Number of Values}$$

Example: The average daily temperature for the first week in January was 31 degrees. If the average temperature for the first 6 days was 30 degrees, what was the temperature on the seventh day?

The sum for all 7 days is $31 \times 7 = 217$ degrees.

The sum of the first 6 days is $30 \times 6 = 180$ degrees.

The temperature on the seventh day is $217 - 180 = 37$ degrees.

For evenly spaced numbers, the average is the middle value. The average of consecutive integers 6, 7, and 8 is 7. The average of 5, 10, 15, and 20 is 12.5 (midway between the middle values 10 and 15).

It might be useful to try to think of the average as the "balanced" value. In other words, the total deficit of all the values below the average will balance out the total surplus of all the values that exceed the average. The average of 3, 5, and 10 is 6. Three is 3 less than 6 and 5 is 1 less than 6, for a total deficit of $3 + 1 = 4$. This is the same amount by which 10 is greater than 6.

Example: The average of 3, 4, 5, and x is 5. What is the value of x?

Think of each value in terms of its position relative to the average, 5.

> 3 is 2 less than the average.
>
> 4 is 1 less than the average.
>
> 5 is at the average.
>
> Together, the three numerical terms have a total deficit of $1 + 2 + 0 = 3$. Therefore, x must be 3 **more** than the average to restore the balance at 5. So x is $3 + 5 = 8$.

Median

On the ACT you might see a reference to the **median**. If a group of numbers is arranged in numerical order, the median is the middle value if there are an odd number of terms in the set or the average of the two middle terms if there is an even number of terms in the set. The median of the numbers 1, 4, 5, 6, and 100 is 5, while the median of the numbers 2, 3, 7, 9, 22, and 34 is $\frac{7+9}{2} = \frac{16}{2} = 8$.

Example: What is the median of the following list of terms: 5, 101, 53, 2, 8, 4, and 11?

> Rearranged in numerical order, the list is 2, 4, 5, 8, 11, 53, and 101. The list contains an odd number of terms, 7, so the median is the middle number, or 8.

In an evenly spaced list of numbers, such as a set of consecutive integers, the median is equal to the mean. However, the median can also be quite different from the mean as you've seen from the examples above.

Mode

The **mode** is rarely tested on the ACT. It refers to the term that appears most frequently in a set. If Set $A = \{1, 5, 7, 1, 3, 4, 1, 3, 0\}$, the mode would be 1 as it shows up 3 times—more than any other term.

If more than one term is tied for most frequent, every one of them is a mode.

Example: What is the mode of the following list of terms: 3, 23, 12, 23, 3, 7, 0, 5?

Both 3 and 23 each appear twice, which is more often than any other term, so both 3 and 23 are modes of this list.

If no term shows up more than once, there is no mode.

Probability

Probability measures the likelihood of an event taking place. It can be expressed as a fraction ("The probability of snow tomorrow is $\frac{1}{2}$"), a decimal ("There is a 0.5 chance of snow tomorrow"), or a percent ("The probability of snow tomorrow is 50%").

When expressed as a fraction, a probability can be read as "x chances in y," where x is the numerator and y is the denominator. So a $\frac{2}{3}$ probability of winning a car could be read as "2 chances in 3 to win a car."

To compute a probability, divide the number of desired outcomes by the number of possible outcomes.

$$\text{Probability} = \frac{\text{Number of Desired Outcomes}}{\text{Number of Possible Outcomes}}$$

Example: If you have 12 shirts in a drawer and 9 of them are white, what is the probability of picking a white shirt at random?

When picking a shirt in this situation, there are 12 possible outcomes, 1 for each shirt. Of these 12, 9 of them are white, so there are 9 desired outcomes.

Therefore, the probability of picking a white shirt at random is $\frac{9}{12} = \frac{3}{4}$. The probability can also be expressed as 0.75 or 75%.

A probability of 0 means that the event has no chance of happening. A probability of 1 means that the event will always happen.

Number Line and Absolute Value

A **number line** is a straight line that extends infinitely in either direction, on which real numbers are represented as points.

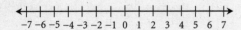

As you move to the right on a number line, the values increase.

Conversely, as you move to the left, the values decrease.

Zero separates the positive numbers (to the right of zero) and the negative numbers (to the left of zero) along the number line. Zero is neither positive nor negative.

The **absolute value** of a number is just the number without its sign. It is written as two vertical lines.

> **Example:** $|-3| = |+3| = 3$

The absolute value can be thought of as the number's distance from zero on the number line. In the example, -3 and 3 are both 3 units from zero, so their absolute values are both 3.

ELEMENTARY ALGEBRA

Elementary algebra will build on some of the concepts introduced in pre-algebra while introducing some new ones as well. The following concepts are important to know for Test Day.

Rules of Operations with Powers

In the term $3x^2$, 3 is the **coefficient**, x is the **base**, and 2 is the **exponent**. The exponent refers to the number of times the base is a factor of the expression. For example, 4^3 has 3 factors of 4 as $4^3 = 4 \times 4 \times 4$.

An integer times itself is the **square** of that integer. ($y \times y$ is the square of y, or y^2)

An integer times itself twice is the **cube** of that integer. ($4 \times 4 \times 4$ is the cube of 4, or 4^3)

To multiply two terms with the same base, keep the base and add the exponents.

$$m^4 \times m^7 = m^{4+7} = m^{11}$$

Example:

$$2^2 \times 2^3 = (2 \times 2)(2 \times 2 \times 2) \qquad \text{or} \qquad 2^2 \times 2^3 = 2^{2+3}$$
$$= (2 \times 2 \times 2 \times 2 \times 2) \qquad\qquad\qquad = 2^5$$
$$= 2^5$$

To divide two terms with the same base, keep the base and subtract the exponent of the denominator from the exponent of the numerator.

$$d^{10} \div d^7 = d^{10-7} = d^3$$

Example:

$$4^4 \div 4^2 = \frac{4 \times 4 \times 4 \times 4}{4 \times 4} \qquad\qquad\qquad 4^4 \div 4^2 = 4^{4-2}$$
$$= \frac{4 \times 4}{1} \qquad \text{or} \qquad\qquad = 4^2$$
$$= 4^2$$

KAPLAN

To raise a power to another power, multiply the exponents.

$$(p^5)^3 = p^{5 \times 3} = p^{15}$$

Example:

$$(3^2)^4 = (3 \times 3)^4$$
$$= (3 \times 3)(3 \times 3)(3 \times 3)(3 \times 3) \qquad \text{or} \qquad (3^2)^4 = 3^{2 \times 4}$$
$$= 3^8 \qquad\qquad\qquad\qquad\qquad\qquad\qquad = 3^8$$

Any nonzero number raised to the zero power is equal to 1. $a^0 = 1$ as long as $a \neq 0$. 0^0 is undefined.

To evaluate a negative exponent, take the reciprocal of the base and change the sign of the exponent.

$$a^{-n} = \frac{1}{a^n} \text{ or } \left(\frac{1}{a}\right)^n$$

Example: $2^{-3} = \left(\frac{1}{2}\right)^3 = \frac{1}{2^3} = \frac{1}{8}$

A fractional exponent indicates a **root**.

$(a)^{\frac{1}{n}} = \sqrt[n]{a}$ (Read "the *n*th root of *a*." If no "*n*" is present, the radical sign means a square root.)

Example: $8^{\frac{1}{3}} = \sqrt[3]{8} = 2$

Rules of Operations with Roots

When it comes to the four basic arithmetic operations, we treat radicals in much the same way we would treat variables.

Addition and Subtraction: Only like radicals can be added to or subtracted from one another.

Example:

$$2\sqrt{3} + 4\sqrt{2} - \sqrt{2} - 3\sqrt{3} = \left(4\sqrt{2} - \sqrt{2}\right) + \left(2\sqrt{3} - 3\sqrt{3}\right) \left[\text{Note: } \sqrt{2} = 1\sqrt{2}\right]$$
$$= 3\sqrt{2} + (-\sqrt{3})$$
$$= 3\sqrt{2} - \sqrt{3}$$

Multiplication and Division: To multiply or divide one radical by another, multiply or divide the numbers outside the radical signs separate from the numbers inside the radical signs, much like you would with coefficients and variables.

Example: $(6\sqrt{3}) \times (2\sqrt{5}) = (6 \times 2)(\sqrt{3} \times \sqrt{5}) = 12\sqrt{3 \times 5} = 12\sqrt{15}$

Example: $12\sqrt{15} \div 2\sqrt{5} = (12 \div 2)(\sqrt{15} \div \sqrt{5}) = 6\left(\dfrac{\sqrt{15}}{\sqrt{5}}\right) = 6\sqrt{3}$

Example: $\dfrac{4\sqrt{18}}{2\sqrt{6}} = \left(\dfrac{4}{2}\right)\left(\dfrac{\sqrt{18}}{\sqrt{6}}\right) = 2\left(\sqrt{\dfrac{18}{6}}\right) = 2\sqrt{3}$

If the number inside the radical is a multiple of a perfect square, the expression can be simplified by factoring out the perfect square.

Example: $\sqrt{72} = \sqrt{36 \times 2} = \sqrt{36} \times \sqrt{2} = 6\sqrt{2}$

Elementary Algebra on the ACT will also move beyond the realm of simple numbers by introducing variables. The following is important to know when dealing with variables.

Algebraic Terminology

Terms: A **term** is a numerical constant or the product (or quotient) of a numerical constant and one or more variables. Examples of terms are $3x$, $4x^2yz$, and $\dfrac{2a}{c}$.

Expressions: An **algebraic expression** is a combination of one or more terms. Terms in an expression are separated by either + or − signs. Examples of expressions are $3xy$, $4ab + 5cd$, and $x^2 - 1$.

A number without any variables is called a **constant term**.

In the term $3xy$, the constant term **3** is called a **coefficient**.

In a simple term where no coefficient is listed, such as z, **1** is the coefficient.

An expression with one term, such as $3xy$, is called a **monomial.**

An expression with two terms, such as $4a + 2d$, is a **binomial.**

An expression with three terms, such as $xy + z - a$, is a **trinomial.**

The general name for expressions with more than one term is **polynomial.**

Operations with Polynomials

All of the laws of arithmetic operations, such as the commutative, associative, and distributive laws, are applicable to polynomials as well.

Commutative law: $2x + 5y = 5y + 2x$

                              $5a \times 3b = 3b \times 5a = 15ab$

Associative law: $(2x + 3x) + 5x = 2x + (3x + 5x) = 10x$

                              $4s \times (7j \times 9p) = (4s \times 7j) \times 2p = 56sjp$

Distributive law: $3a(2b - 5c) = (3a \times 2b) - (3a + 2b) - (3a \times 5c) = 6ab - 15ac$

KAPLAN

Note: The product of two binomials can be calculated by applying the distributive law twice.

Example:

$$(x + 5)(x - 2) = x(x - 2) + 5(x - 2)$$
$$= x \times x - x \times 2 + 5 \times x - 5 \times 2$$
$$= x^2 - 2x + 5x - 10$$
$$= x^2 - 3x - 10$$

A simple mnemonic for this is **F**irst **O**uter **I**nner **L**ast, or **FOIL**.

Factoring Algebraic Expressions

Factoring a polynomial means expressing it as a product of two or more simpler expressions.

Common monomial factor: When there is a monomial factor common to every term in the polynomial, it can be factored out by using the distributive law.

Example: $2a + 6ac = 2a(1 + 3c)$ ($2a$ is the greatest common factor of $2a$ and $6ac$)

Difference of two perfect squares: The difference of two squares can be factored into a product: $a^2 - b^2 = (a - b)(a + b)$

Example: $9x^2 - 1 = (3x)^2 - (1)^2 = (3x + 1)(3x - 1)$

Polynomials of the form $a^2 + 2ab + b^2$: Any polynomial of this form is equivalent to the square of a binomial. Notice that $(a + b)^2 = a^2 + 2ab + b^2$ (try FOIL).

Factoring such a polynomial is just reversing this procedure.

Example: $x^2 + 6x + 9 = (x)^2 + 2(x)(3) + (3)^2 = (x + 3)^2$

Polynomials of the form $a^2 - 2ab + b^2$: Any polynomial of this form is equivalent to the square of a binomial as well. Here, though, the binomial is the difference of two terms: $(a - b)^2 = a^2 - 2ab + b^2$.

Example: $x^2 - 4x + 4 = (x)^2 - 2(x)(2) + (2)^2 = (x - 2)^2$

Polynomials of the form $ax^2 + bx + c$: Polynomials of this form can nearly always be factored into a product of two binomials. The product of the first terms in each binomial must equal the first term of the polynomial. The product of the last terms of the binomials must equal the third term of the polynomial. The sum of the remaining products must equal the second term of the polynomial. Factoring can be thought of as the FOIL method backwards.

Example: $x^2 - 3x + 2$

We can factor this into two binomials, each containing an x term. Start by writing down what we know.

$x^2 - 3x + 2 = (x)(x)$

We need to fill in the missing term to the right of each binomial. The **product** of the two missing terms will be the last term in the polynomial: 2. The **sum** of the two missing terms will be the coefficient of the second term of the polynomial: –3. Try the possible factors of 2 until we get a pair that adds up to –3. There are two possibilities: 1 and 2, or –1 and –2. Since $(-1) + (-2) = -3$, we can fill –1 and –2 into the empty spaces.

Thus, $x^2 - 3x + 2 = (x - 1)(x - 2)$.

Note: Using FOIL on a factored polynomial is a great way to check your work.

Inequalities

Inequality symbols:

> greater than

< less than

≥ greater than or equal to

≤ less than or equal to

Example: $x > 4$ means all numbers greater than 4

Example: $x < 0$ means all numbers less than zero (the negative numbers)

Example: $x \geq -2$ means x can be –2 or any number greater than –2

Example: $x \leq \frac{1}{2}$ means x can be $\frac{1}{2}$ or any number less than $\frac{1}{2}$.

Solving Inequalities: Inequalities behave the same way as normal equations with one exception:

Multiplying or dividing by a negative number reverses the inequality's direction.

Example: $-1(-3x < 2) = 3x > -2$

Example: Solve for x and represent the solution set on a number line: $3 - \frac{x}{4} \geq 2$

1. Multiply both sides by 4.
2. Subtract 12 from both sides.
3. Divide both sides by –1 and change the direction of the sign. $x \leq 4$

KAPLAN

Note: The solution set to an inequality is not a single value but a range of possible values. Here, the values include 4 and all numbers below 4.

INTERMEDIATE ALGEBRA

Intermediate algebra continues to build upon the concepts introduced thus far while adding several more advanced ones. The following will be important to know for the ACT.

Simultaneous Equations

Sometimes a problem on the ACT will involve an equation with more than one variable. In general, if you want to find numerical values for all your variables, you will need as many **distinct** equations as you have variables. Two equations are **distinct** if neither simplifies into the other. $x^2 + 2xy + 5y^2 = 5$ and $3x^2 + 6xy + 15y^2 = 15$ are *not* distinct since multiplying the first equation by 3 results in the second.

If we had one equation with two variables, such as $x - y = 7$, there are an infinite number of solution sets since each unique value of x has a different corresponding value for y. If $x = 8$, $y = 1$ (since $8 - 1 = 7$). If $x = 12$, $y = 5$ (since $12 - 5 = 7$). And so forth.

If we are given two **distinct** equations with two variables, we can combine them to get a unique solution set. This is known as a **system of equations**. There are two ways to do this:

Method I: Combination

Combination involves subtracting a multiple, positive or negative, of one equation from the other. The idea is to choose a multiple such that all but one of the variables is eliminated, solve for that variable, then plug that variable back into the *other* equation for the other variable if necessary.

> **Example:** If $3a + 2b = 12$ and $5a + 4b = 23$, what is the value of a?
>
> 1. Start by lining up the equations, one under the other. $3a + 2b = 12$
> $5a + 4b = 23$
>
> 2. Multiply the top equation by 2, to get $4b$ in both. $6a + 4b = 24$
> $5a + 4b = 23$
>
> 3. Subtract to eliminate the b term. $6a + 4b = 24$
> $- (5a + 4b = 23)$
> $a = 1$

Method II: Substitution

Substitution involves solving for one of the variables in terms of the other in one equation, then substituting that value back into the other equation.

Example: Solve for m and n when $m = 4n + 2$ and $3m + 2n = 16$.

1. We have m in terms of n so substitute $4n + 2$ for m in the second equation.

$$3(4n + 2) + 2n = 16$$
$$12n + 6 + 2n = 16$$

2. Solve for n.

$$14n = 10$$
$$n = \frac{10}{14} = \frac{5}{7}$$

3. Substitute $\frac{5}{7}$ for n in the first equation to solve for m.

$$m = 4n + 2$$
$$m = 4\left(\frac{5}{7}\right) + 2$$
$$= \frac{20}{7} + \frac{14}{7}$$
$$= \frac{34}{7}$$

Quadratic Equations

When the polynomial $ax^2 + bx + c$ equals 0, it is given a special name—a **quadratic equation**. As an equation, we can find the value(s) of x that make it true.

Example: $x^2 - 3x + 2 = 0$

To find the solutions, or roots, start by doing what we did earlier in this chapter—factor it. We can factor $x^2 - 3x + 2$ into $(x - 2)(x - 1)$, making our quadratic equation $(x - 2)(x - 1) = 0$.

We now have an equation where the product of two binomials equals 0. This can only be the case when at least one of the terms is 0. Therefore, to find the roots, we just need to set the two binomials equal to 0 and solve for x. In other words, either $x - 2 = 0$ or $x - 1 = 0$ (or both.) Solving for x, we get $x = 2$ or $x = 1$. To check the math, plug 1 and 2 back into the original equation and make sure that both variables satisfy the equation.

$2^2 - 3(2) + 2 = 0$	$1^2 - 3(1) + 2 = 0$
$4 - 6 + 2 = 0$	$1 - 3 + 2 = 0$
$0 = 0$	$0 = 0$

Functions

Classic function notation problems may also appear on the ACT. An algebraic expression of only one variable may be defined as a function, f or g, of that variable.

Example: What is the minimum value of the function $f(x) = x^2 - 1$?

In the function $f(x) = x^2 - 1$, if x is 1, then $f(1) = 1^2 - 1 = 0$. In other words, by inputting 1 into the function, the output $f(x) = 0$. Every number inputted has only one output (though the reverse is not necessarily true).

Here, you are asked to find the minimum value, that is, the smallest possible value of the function. Minimums are usually found using math that is much too complex for the ACT, so any minimum (or maximum) value problem on the test can be solved in one of two simple ways: Either plug the answer choices into the function and find which gives you the lowest value, or apply some critical thinking before testing any values. In the case of $f(x) = x^2 - 1$, the function will be at a minimum when x^2 is as small as possible. Since x^2 gets larger the farther x is from 0, x^2 is as small as possible when $x = 0$. Consequently, the smallest value of $x^2 - 1$ occurs when $x = 0$. So the minimum value of the function is $f(0) = 0^2 - 1 = -1$.

Matrices

Matrices do not appear on the ACT test very often and those that do will be very straightforward and simple. Take matrices A and B below:

$$A = \begin{bmatrix} 3 & 4 \\ 6 & 2 \end{bmatrix} \quad B = \begin{bmatrix} 1 & 2 \\ 5 & 7 \end{bmatrix}$$

To add or subtract matrices, simply add or subtract the corresponding number. $A + B$ would be:

$$\begin{bmatrix} 3+1 & 4+2 \\ 6+5 & 2+7 \end{bmatrix} = \begin{bmatrix} 4 & 6 \\ 11 & 9 \end{bmatrix}$$

This is the extent of any matrix problems you might see on the ACT.

PLANE GEOMETRY

Plane geometry deals with a broad range of topics. The following is a list of what you can expect to see on the ACT.

Lines and Angles

A line is a one-dimensional geometric abstraction—infinitely long with no width. It is not physically possible to **draw** a line as any physical line would have a finite length and some width, no matter how long and thin we tried to make it. Two points determine a straight line: Given any two points, there is exactly one straight line that passes through them.

Lines: A **line segment** is a section of a straight line of finite length with two endpoints. A line segment is named for its endpoints, as in segment AB. The **midpoint** is the point that divides a line segment into two equal parts.

Example: In the figure above, A and B are the endpoints of $\overline{AB}$ and M is its midpoint ($\overline{AM} = \overline{MB}$). What is the length of AB? $\overline{AM}$ is 6, meaning $\overline{MB}$ is also 6, so $\overline{AB} = 6 + 6 = 12$.

Two lines are **parallel** if they lie on the same plane and will never intersect each other regardless of how far they are extended. If line l_1 is parallel to line l_2, we write $l_1 || l_2$.

Angles: An **angle** is formed whenever two lines or line segments intersect at a point. The point of intersection is called the **vertex** of the angle. Angles are measured in degrees (°).

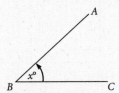

Angle x, $\angle ABC$, and $\angle B$ all denote the same angle in the diagram above.

An **acute angle** is an angle whose degree measure is between 0° and 90°. A **right angle** is an angle whose degree measure is exactly 90°. An **obtuse angle** is an angle whose degree measure is between 90° and 180°. A **straight angle** is an angle whose degree measure is exactly 180°.

| acute $(x < 90)$ | right $(y = 90)$ | obtuse $(90 < z < 180)$ | straight $(w = 180)$ |

The sum of the measures of the angles on one side of a straight line is 180°.

straight
$(x + y + z = 180)$

The sum of the measures of the angles around a point is 360°.

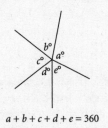

$a + b + c + d + e = 360$

Two lines are **perpendicular** if they intersect at a 90° angle. The shortest distance from a point to a line is the line segment drawn from the point to the line such that it is perpendicular to the line. If line l_1 is perpendicular to line l_2, we write $l_1 \perp l_2$. If $l_1 \perp l_2$ and $l_2 \perp l_3$ then $l_1 \| l_2$:

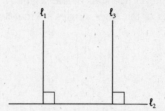

Two angles are **supplementary** if together they make up a straight angle, i.e., if the sum of their measures is 180°. Two angles are **complementary** if together they make up a right angle, i.e., if the sum of their measures is 90°.

A line or line segment **bisects** an angle if it splits the angle into two equal halves. $\overline{BD}$ below bisects $\angle ABC$, and $\angle ABD$ has the same measure as $\angle DBC$. The two smaller angles are each half the size of $\angle ABC$.

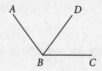

Vertical angles are a pair of opposite angles formed by two intersecting line segments. At the point of intersection, two pairs of vertical angles are formed. Angles a and c below are vertical angles, as are b and d.

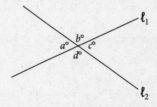

The two angles in a pair of vertical angles have the same degree measure. In the diagram above, $a = c$ and $b = d$. In addition, since l_1 and l_2 are straight lines, $a + b = c + d = a + d = b + c = 180$. In other words, each angle is supplementary to each of its two adjacent angles.

If two parallel lines intersect with a third line (called a *transversal*), each of the parallel lines will intersect the third line at the same angle. In the figure below, $a = e$ (corresponding angles in a transversal), $a = c$ (vertical angles), and $e = g$ (vertical angles). Therefore, $a = c = e = g$ and $b = d = f = h$.

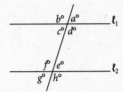

If $l_1 \| l_2$, then $a = c = e = g$ and $b = d = f = h$.

In other words, when two parallel lines intersect with a third line, all acute angles formed are equal, all obtuse angles formed are equal, and any acute angle is supplementary to any obtuse angle.

Triangles

General Triangles

A **triangle** is a closed figure with three angles and three straight sides.

> The sum of the measures of the angles in a triangle is 180°.

Each interior angle is supplementary to an adjacent **exterior angle**. The degree measure of an exterior angle is equal to the sum of the measures of the two nonadjacent (remote) interior angles, or 180° minus the measure of the adjacent interior angle.

In the figure below, a, b, and c are interior angles, so $a + b + c = 180$. d is supplementary to c as well, so $d + c = 180$, $d + c = a + b + c$, and $d = a + b$. Thus, the exterior angle d is equal to the sum of the two remote interior angles—a and b.

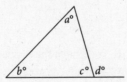

The **altitude** (or height) of a triangle is the perpendicular distance from a vertex to the side opposite the vertex. The altitude can fall inside the triangle, outside the triangle, or on one of the sides.

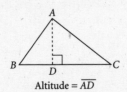

Altitude = $\overline{AD}$

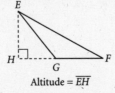

Altitude = $\overline{EH}$

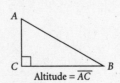

Altitude = $\overline{AC}$

Sides and angles: The length of any side of a triangle is less than the sum of the lengths of the other two sides and greater than their positive difference.

$$b + c > a > b - c$$
$$a + b > c > a - b$$
$$a + c > b > a - c$$

If the lengths of two sides of a triangle are unequal, the **greater angle** lies **opposite the longer side** and vice versa. In the figure above, if $\angle A > \angle B > \angle C$ then $a > b > c$.

Area of a triangle: The **area** of a triangle refers to the space it takes up.

Example: The triangle below has a base of 4 and an altitude of 3, so we write:

> The area of a triangle is $\frac{1}{2}$ base × height.

$$A = \frac{1}{2}bh$$
$$= \frac{1}{2} \times 4 \times 3 = 6$$

Remember that the height (or altitude) is perpendicular to the base. Therefore, when two sides of a triangle are perpendicular to each other, the area is easy to find. In a right triangle, we call the two sides that form the 90° angle the **legs**. Then the area is one-half the product of the legs:

$$A = \frac{1}{2}bh$$

$$= \frac{1}{2}l_1 \times l_2$$

Example: In the triangle below, we could treat the hypotenuse as the base, since that's how the figure is drawn. If we did this, we would need to know the distance from the hypotenuse to the opposite vertex in order to determine the area of the triangle. A more straightforward method is to notice that this is a **right** triangle with legs of lengths 6 and 8, which allows us to use the alternative formula for the area:

$$A = \frac{1}{2}l_1 \times l_2 = \frac{1}{2} \times 6 \times 8 = 24$$

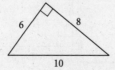

Perimeter of a triangle: The **perimeter** of a triangle is the distance around the triangle. In other words, the perimeter is equal to the sum of the lengths of the sides.

> **Example:** In the triangle below, the sides are of length 5, 6, and 8. Therefore, the perimeter is 5 + 6 + 8, or 19.

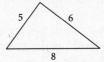

Isosceles triangles: An **isosceles triangle** is a triangle that has two sides of equal length. The two equal sides are called the **legs** and the third side is called the **base**.

Since the two legs have the same length, the two angles opposite the legs must have the same measure. In the figure below, $\overline{PQ} = \overline{PR}$ and $\angle R = \angle Q$.

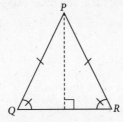

Equilateral triangles: An **equilateral triangle** has three sides of equal length and three 60° angles.

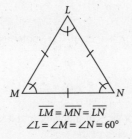

$$\overline{LM} = \overline{MN} = \overline{LN}$$
$$\angle L = \angle M = \angle N = 60°$$

Similar triangles: Triangles are **similar** if they have the same shape—if corresponding angles have the same measure. For instance, any two triangles whose angles measure 30°, 60°, and 90° are similar. In similar triangles, corresponding sides are in the same ratio. Triangles are **congruent** if corresponding angles have the same measure and corresponding sides have the same length.

> **Example:** What is the perimeter of $\triangle DEF$ below?

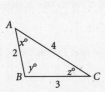 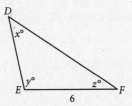

Each triangle has an $x°$ angle, a $y°$ angle, and a $z°$ angle, so they are similar and corresponding sides are in the same ratio. $\overline{BC}$ and $\overline{EF}$ are corresponding sides—each is opposite the $x°$ angle. Since $\overline{EF}$ is twice the length of $\overline{BC}$, **each** side of $\triangle DEF$ will be twice the length of its corresponding side in $\triangle ABC$.

Therefore, $\overline{DE} = 2(\overline{AB}) = 4$ and $\overline{DF} = 2(\overline{AC}) = 8$. The perimeter of $\triangle DEF$ is $4 + 6 + 8 = 18$.

The ratio of the **areas** of two similar triangles is the **square** of the ratio of their corresponding lengths. In the example above, since each side of $\triangle DEF$ is twice the length of its corresponding side in $\triangle ABC$, the area of $\triangle DEF$ must be $2^2 = 4$ times the area of $\triangle ABC$.

$$\frac{Area\ \triangle DEF}{Area\ \triangle ABC} = \left(\frac{DE}{AB}\right)^2 = \left(\frac{2}{1}\right)^2 = 4$$

Right triangles: A right triangle has one interior angle of 90°. The longest side, which lies opposite the right angle, is called the **hypotenuse**. The other two sides are called the **legs**.

Pythagorean Theorem

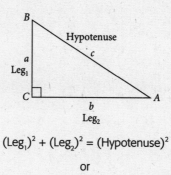

$$(Leg_1)^2 + (Leg_2)^2 = (Hypotenuse)^2$$

or

$$a^2 + b^2 = c^2$$

The **Pythagorean Theorem** holds for all right triangles, and it states that the square of the hypotenuse is equal to the sum of the squares of the legs.

Some sets of integers happen to satisfy the Pythagorean Theorem. These sets of integers are commonly referred to as **Pythagorean triplets**. One very common set that you might remember is 3, 4, and 5. Since $3^2 + 4^2 = 5^2$, if you have a right triangle with legs of lengths 3 and 4, the length of the hypotenuse would have to be 5. This is the most common kind of right triangle on the ACT, though the sides are generally presented as a multiple of 3, 4, and 5, such as 6, 8, and 10, or 12, 16, and 20. Memorize this ratio and you'll be well on your way to speeding by triangle problems that feature this triplet on the ACT. Another triplet that occasionally appears on the ACT is 5, 12, and 13.

Whenever you're given the lengths of two sides of a right triangle, the Pythagorean Theorem allows you to find the third side.

Example: What is the length of the hypotenuse of a right triangle with legs of lengths 9 and 10?

The Pythagorean Theorem states that the square of the length of the hypotenuse equals the sum of the squares of the lengths of the legs. Here the legs are 9 and 10, so we have

$$\text{Hypotenuse}^2 = 9^2 + 10^2$$
$$= 81 + 100$$
$$= 181$$
$$\text{Hypotenuse} = \sqrt{181}$$

Example: What is the length of the hypotenuse of an isosceles right triangle with legs of length 4?

Since we're told the triangle is isosceles, we know two of the sides have the same length. We know the hypotenuse can't be the same length as one of the legs (the hypotenuse must be the longest side), so it must be that the two legs are equal. Therefore, the two legs each have length 4, and we can use the Pythagorean Theorem to find the hypotenuse.

$$\text{Hypotenuse}^2 = 4^2 + 4^2$$
$$= 16 + 16$$
$$= 32$$
$$\text{Hypotenuse} = \sqrt{32}$$
$$= \sqrt{16} \times \sqrt{2}$$
$$= 4\sqrt{2}$$

You can always use the Pythagorean Theorem to find the lengths of the sides in a right triangle. There are, however, two special kinds of right triangles that always have the same ratios.

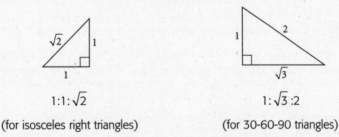

$1:1:\sqrt{2}$ $1:\sqrt{3}:2$

(for isosceles right triangles)   (for 30-60-90 triangles)

These two types of special right triangles are tested often enough that it is to your benefit to memorize these proportions as that would allow you to blow past such problems without having to do any math. If you forget them on Test Day, rest assured that you can still solve the problem with the Pythagorean Theorem (it would just take longer).

Polygons

A **polygon** is a closed figure whose sides are straight line segments.

The **perimeter** of a polygon is the sum of the lengths of its sides.

A **vertex** of a polygon is the point where two adjacent sides meet.

A **diagonal** of a polygon is a line segment connecting two nonadjacent vertices.

A **regular polygon** has sides of equal length and interior angles of equal measure.

The number of sides determines the specific name of the polygon. A **triangle** has three sides, a **quadrilateral** has four sides, a **pentagon** has five sides, and a **hexagon** has six sides. Triangles and quadrilaterals are by far the most important polygons on the ACT.

Interior and exterior angles: A polygon can be divided into triangles by drawing diagonals from a given vertex to all other nonadjacent vertices. For instance, the pentagon below can be divided into three triangles. Since the sum of the interior angles of each triangle is 180°, the sum of the interior angles of a pentagon is $3 \times 180° = 540°$.

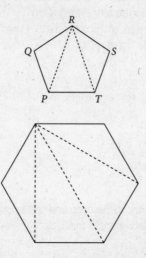

Example: What is the measure of an interior angle in the regular hexagon above?

All angles are equal, so each is equal to one-sixth the sum of the angles. Since we can draw four triangles in a six-sided figure, the sum of the interior angles is $4 \times 180° = 720°$. Therefore, each angle measures $\frac{720}{6} = 120°$.

The formula to represent the total measure of an n-sided polygon's interior angles is $180(n - 2)$.

Quadrilaterals

While there are many quadrilaterals in math, the only two that you need to worry about are **rectangles** and **squares**.

A **rectangle** is a quadrilateral with two sets of parallel sides and four right angles.

A **square** is an equilateral **rectangle**.

Note the following formulas for Test Day:

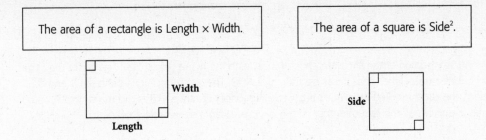

| The area of a rectangle is Length × Width. | The area of a square is Side². |

Circles

Circle: The set of all points in a plane at the same distance from a certain point. This point is called the **focus** and lies at the **center** of the circle.

A circle is labeled by its center point: circle *O* means the circle with center point *O*. Two circles of different size with the same center are **concentric**.

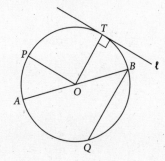

Diameter: A line segment that connects two points on the circle and passes through the center of the circle. In circle *O*, $\overline{AB}$ is a diameter.

Radius: A line segment from the center of the circle to any point on the circle. The radius of a circle is one-half the length of its diameter. In circle *O*, $\overline{OA}$, $\overline{OB}$, $\overline{OP}$, and $\overline{OT}$ are all radii.

Chord: A line segment joining two points on the circle. In circle *O*, $\overline{QB}$ *and* $\overline{AB}$ are chords. The longest chord in a circle is a diameter.

Central angle: An angle formed by two radii. ∠*AOP*, ∠*POB*, and ∠*BOA* are three of circle *O*'s central angles.

Tangent: A line that touches only one point on the circumference of the circle. A line drawn tangent to a circle is perpendicular to the radius at the point of tangency. Line *l* is tangent to circle *O* at point *T*.

Circumference and arc length: The distance around a circle is its **circumference**. The number π ("pi") is the ratio of a circle's circumference to its diameter. The value of π is usually approximated to 3.14. For the ACT, it is generally sufficient to remember that π is a little more than 3.

Since π equals the ratio of the circumference to the diameter, a formula for the circumference is

$$\text{Circumference} = \pi d = 2\pi r$$

An **arc** is a portion of the circumference of a circle. In the figure below, *AB* is an arc of the circle, with the same degree measure as central angle *AOB*. The shorter distance between *A* and *B* along the circle is called the **minor arc**, while the longer distance *AXB* is the **major arc**. An arc that is exactly half the circumference of the circle is called a **semicircle** (meaning half a circle).

The length of an arc is the same fraction of a circle's circumference as its degree measure is of the degree measure of the circle (360°). For an arc with a central angle measuring *n* degrees, the following applies:

$$\text{Arc length} = \left(\frac{n}{360}\right)(\text{circumference})$$

$$= \frac{n}{360} \times 2\pi r$$

Example: What is the length of arc *ABC* of the circle with center *O* above?

The radius is 6, so the circumference is $2\pi r = 2 \times \pi \times 6 = 12\pi$.

Since $\angle AOC$ measures 60°, the arc is $\frac{60}{360} = \frac{1}{6}$ the circumference.

Therefore, the length of the arc is $\frac{12\pi}{6} = 2\pi$.

Area of a circle: The area of a circle is given by the formula

$$\text{Area} = \pi r^2$$

A **sector** is a portion of a circle bounded by two radii and an arc. In the circle below with center *O, OAB* is a sector. To determine the area of a sector of a circle, use the same method we used to find the length of an arc. Determine what fraction of 360° is in the degree measure of the central angle of the sector, then multiply that fraction by the area of the circle. In a sector whose central angle measures *n* degrees, the following applies:

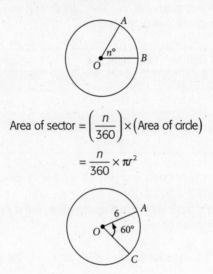

$$\text{Area of sector} = \left(\frac{n}{360}\right) \times \left(\text{Area of circle}\right)$$

$$= \frac{n}{360} \times \pi r^2$$

Example: What is the area of sector *AOC* in the circle above?

A 60° "slice" is $\dfrac{60}{360} = \dfrac{1}{6}$ of the circle, so sector *AOC* has an area of

$$\frac{1}{6} \times \pi r^2 = \frac{1}{6} \times \pi \times 6^2 = \frac{1}{6} \times 36\pi = 6\pi.$$

COORDINATE GEOMETRY

As indicated by its name, coordinate geometry is geometry on the coordinate plane. This mostly includes equations and graphs of lines, circles, and triangles.

The important formulas to remember for lines are the following:

1. Slope-Intercept Formula: $y = mx + b$, where *m* is the slope and *b* is the y-intercept of the line.

2. Midpoint formula: The midpoint of a line segment bounded by the points (x_1, y_1), (x_2, y_2) is
$$\left(\frac{x_1 + x_2}{2}, \frac{y_1 + y_2}{2}\right).$$

3. Distance Formula: The distance between two points (x_1, y_1), (x_2, y_2) is
$$D = \sqrt{(x_2 - x_1)^2 + (y_2 - y_1)^2}.$$

When dealing with parallel and perpendicular lines, remember that parallel lines have the same slope and perpendicular lines have opposite reciprocal slopes. Also, remember that horizontal lines have a slope of zero and vertical lines have a slope that is undefined.

The same equations for circles described above in plane geometry also apply to coordinate geometry. Additionally, you should also know how to relate the equations to the graphs and how to graph inequalities. A good way to deal with linear inequalities is to simply replace the inequality sign with an equal sign and graph the line. Then, depending on what inequality sign the problem uses, shade the appropriate side of the line.

If the inequality sign is:	Line included:	Shaded Area:
<	No	Below line
>	No	Above line
≤	Yes	Below line
≥	Yes	Above line

Commit these relationships to memory and you will be able to solve inequality problems quickly.

You should also know some basic graphs that may appear on the ACT. These include the common conic graphs, parabolas, and circles.

A **parabola** is the graph of a quadratic function, such as $y = x^2$. The graph of a parabola looks like this:

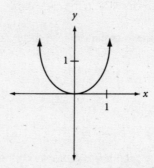

The equation of a circle is $(x - h)^2 + (y - k)^2 = r^2$, where r is the radius of the circle and (h, k) is its center.

The equation of an ellipse is $\dfrac{(x - h)^2}{a^2} + \dfrac{(y - k)^2}{b^2} = r^2$, where a represents half of the horizontal axis and b represents half of the vertical axis.

TRIGONOMETRY

Trigonometry can seem intimidating as it is a fairly advanced math subject, but the ACT only tests the very basics of it.

The basic trigonometry functions are the sine, cosine, and tangent functions. These can be remembered using the SOHCOHTOA mnemonic device.

The sine function: $\quad sin\theta = \dfrac{opposite}{hypotenuse}$

The cosine function: $\quad cos\theta = \dfrac{adjacent}{hypotenuse}$

The tangent function: $\quad tan\theta = \dfrac{opposite}{adjacent} = \dfrac{sin}{cos\theta}$

Values of the above functions for certain angles should be committed to memory as they appear often.

Angle (°)	Sine	Cosine	Tangent
0	0	1	0
30	1/2	$\dfrac{\sqrt{3}}{2}$	$\dfrac{\sqrt{3}}{3}$
45	$\dfrac{\sqrt{2}}{2}$	$\dfrac{\sqrt{2}}{2}$	1
60	$\dfrac{\sqrt{3}}{2}$	1/2	$\sqrt{3}$
90	1	0	undefined

In addition to these three basic formulas, there are three inverse formulas: secant, cosecant, and tangent.

The secant formula: $\quad sec\theta = \dfrac{1}{cos\theta} = \dfrac{hypotenuse}{adjacent}$

The cosecant formula: $\quad csc\theta = \dfrac{1}{sin\theta} = \dfrac{hypotenuse}{opposite}$

The cotangent formula: $\quad cot\theta = \dfrac{1}{tan\theta} = \dfrac{cos\theta}{sin\theta}$

There are also some trigonometric identities that you should be familiar with. The most common are the Pythagorean identities:

$sin^2\theta + cos^2\theta = 1$

$1 + tan^2\theta = sec^2\theta$

$1 + cot^2\theta = csc^2\theta$

KAPLAN

Chapter Five: **Pre-Algebra Practice**

PRACTICE QUESTIONS

1. What is the average of 230, 155, 320, 400, and 325?

   A. 205
   B. 286
   C. 300
   D. 430

2. Sarah has a wooden board that is 12 feet long. If she cuts three 28-inch pieces from the board, how much board will she have left?

   F. 14 inches
   G. 28 inches
   H. 36 inches
   J. 60 inches

3. If $4x + 18 = 38$, $x =$

   A. 3
   B. 4.5
   C. 5
   D. 12
   E. 20

4. John weighs 1.5 times as much as Ellen. If John weighs 165 lbs., how much does Ellen weigh?

   F. 100 lbs.
   G. 110 lbs.
   H. 150 lbs.
   J. 165 lbs.

5. What is the average of 237, 482, 375, and 210?

    A. 150

    B. 185

    C. 210

    D. 326

6. If $\sqrt[3]{x} = 4$, $x =$

    F. 4

    G. 12

    H. 36

    J. 64

$x = 4^3$

$x = 64$

7. $x^2 + 14 = 63$, $x =$

    A. 4.5

    B. 7

    C. 14

    D. 24.5

$x^2 = 49$

$x = 49^{1/2}$

$x = 7$

$x^2 + 14 = 63$

$-14 \quad -14$

$x^2 = 49$

$x = 49^{1/2}$

$x = 7$

8. Which of the following is equivalent to $\sqrt{54}$?

    F. $2\sqrt{3}$

    G. $3\sqrt{6}$

    H. 15

    J. $9\sqrt{6}$

7.348469228

7.3

9. What whole number is closest to the solution of $\sqrt{90} \times \sqrt{32}$?

    A. 7

    B. 11

    C. 36

    D. 39

9.4   5.6

9.487×5.656

9×6

54

10. $5.2^3 + 6.8^2 =$

    F. 46.24

    G. 94.872

    H. 140.608

    J. 186.848

$140.608 + 46.24$

11. If x is a real number such that $x^3 = 512$, what is the value of x^2?

    A. 8
    B. 16
    C. 64
    D. 135

    $512^{\frac{1}{2}}$

    $x = 8$

    $x^2 = 64$

12. $3^3 \div 9 + (6^2 - 12) \div 4 =$

    F. 3
    G. 6.75
    H. 9
    J. 12

    $3^3 \div 9 + 24 \div 4$

    $27 \div 9 + 24 \div 4$

    $3 + 6$

    9

13. If bananas cost $0.24 and oranges cost $0.38, what is the total cost of x bananas and y oranges?

    A. $(x + y)(\$.24 + \$.38)$
    B. $\$.24x + \$.38y$
    C. $\$.62(x + y)$
    D. $\dfrac{\$.24}{x} + \dfrac{\$.38}{y}$

    $.24x + .38y$

14. If $4x + 13 = 16$, what is the value of x?

    F. 0.25
    G. 0.55
    H. 0.70
    J. 0.75

    $4x = 3$

    $x = \frac{3}{4}$

    $x = .75$

    $4x + 13 = 16$
    $\quad -13 \quad -13$
    $4x = 3$
    $\quad +4 \quad +4$
    $x = 3/4$
    $x = .75$

    $4y + 13 = 16$
    $\quad -13 \quad -13$
    $4x = 3$

15. The chart below shows the total pizza slice sales for a pizza restaurant over a weekend. If pepperoni slices cost $2.45 and cheese slices cost $1.95, how much did the restaurant earn on Friday from pepperoni and cheese slices?

	Friday	Saturday	Sunday
Cheese	38	46	36
Sausage	43	52	47
Pepperoni	41	49	44

    A. $174.55
    B. $178.00
    C. $199.45
    D. $207.80

    100.45
    74.11

    $38(1.95) = 74.10$
    $+$
    $41(2.45) = 100.45$
    $=$
    174.55

16. If $.75x - 13 = 2$, what is the value of x?

    F. 11.25
    G. 14.67
    H. 16
    J. 20

    $.75x = 15$
    $x = 20$

17. In lowest terms, $\frac{3}{7} \times \frac{4}{3} =$

    A. $\frac{9}{28}$

    B. $\frac{7}{21}$

    C. $\frac{3}{7}$

    D. $\frac{4}{7}$

    21 *

ANSWERS AND EXPLANATIONS

1. B

Plug the terms into the average formula and solve:

$$\text{Average} = \frac{\text{sum of terms}}{\text{number of terms}}$$

$$= \frac{230 + 155 + 320 + 400 + 325}{5}$$

$$= \frac{1430}{5}$$

$$= 286$$

That's B.

2. J

Begin by converting Sarah's 12 feet of wood into inches. There are 12 inches in a foot, so Sarah has 12×12 inches = 144 inches. Cutting off three 28-inch pieces removes $3 \times 28 = 84$ inches, which leaves her with $144 - 84 = 60$ inches. That's choice J.

3. C

To evaluate x, isolate it on one side of the equation, then solve.

$$4x + 18 = 38$$

$$4x = 20$$

$$x = 5$$

Choice C is correct.

4. G

Since John weighs *more* than Ellen, begin by eliminating choice J, as doing so will reduce the chance of a miscalculation error. According to the problem, John's 165 lbs. represents 1.5 times Ellen's weight. Therefore, Ellen's weight must be $\frac{165}{1.5} = 110$ lbs. G is correct.

5. D

To find the average of four numbers, plug them into the Average formula and solve:

$$\text{Average} = \frac{\text{sum of terms}}{\text{number of terms}}$$

$$= \frac{237 + 482 + 375 + 210}{4}$$

$$= \frac{1304}{4}$$

$$= 326.$$

Choice D is correct.

6. H

Cube both sides to solve for x:

$$\sqrt[3]{x} = 4$$

$$x = 64$$

7. B

Isolate the variable, then solve for x:

$$x^2 + 14 = 63$$

$$x^2 = 49$$

$$x = \pm 7$$

7 is choice B.

8. G

You *could* use your calculator to solve this problem but there's a much easier way. Begin by eliminating choice H is not a perfect square. J can also be eliminated as $9^2 = 81$, which is way too large. To simplify the radical, factor out a perfect square from 54. The largest factor of 54 that's also a perfect square is 9, so $\sqrt{54} = \sqrt{9 \times 6} = 3\sqrt{6}$

9. D

You *could* punch the expression into your calculator but it may actually be quicker to estimate. $\sqrt{90} \approx \sqrt{81} = 9$ and $\sqrt{32} \approx \sqrt{36} = 6$, so $\sqrt{90} \times \sqrt{32} \approx 9 \times 6 = 54$. With the calculator, the actual value is 53.6656. That's closest to choice D.

10. J

When the choices are spaced far apart, estimation is generally the quickest way to the correct answer. To estimate, round 5.2 to 5 and 6.8 to 7. Since $5^3 + 7^2 = 125 + 49 = 174$, the correct answer will be very close to 174. That would be choice J.

11. C

$x^3 = 512$, so $x = \sqrt[3]{512} = 8$. Be careful not to stop too soon. The problem asks for x^2, not x.
$8^2 = 64$, which is choice C.

12. H

To solve this problem, you'll need to follow the order of operations (PEMDAS).

First, evaluate the parentheses: $3^3 \div 9 + (6^2 - 12) \div 4 = 3^3 \div 9 + (36 - 12) \div 4 = 3^3 \div 9 + 24 \div 4$

Next, simplify the exponent: $3^3 \div 9 + 24 \div 4 = 27 \div 9 + 24 \div 4$

Then, take care of any multiplication and/or division, from left to right: $27 \div 9 + 24 \div 4 = 3 + 6$

Finally, take care of any addition and/or subtraction, from left to right: $3 + 6 = 9$

So H is correct.

13. B

Each banana costs $.24, so the price of x bananas is $.24$x$. Similarly, each orange costs $.38, so the price of y oranges is $.38$y$. Therefore, the total price of x bananas and y oranges is $.24$x$ + $.38$y$. That's B.

14. J

Isolate the variable, then solve for x:

$$4x + 13 = 16$$

$$4x = 3$$

$$x = \frac{3}{4}$$

J is correct.

15. A

Take a moment to familiarize yourself with the table before diving into the problem. The question asks for Friday's pepperoni and cheese sales, so be sure that you are reading data from the correct column. On Friday, 41 pepperoni slices were sold at $2.45 per slice and 38 cheese slices were sold at $1.95 per slice, for sales totaling (2.45×41) + (1.95×38) = $100.45 + $74.10 = $174.55. That's A.

16. J

If the decimal makes this problem seem difficult, convert it into a fraction before solving for x:

$$.75x - 13 = 2$$

$$\frac{3x}{4} = 15$$

$$3x = 60$$

$$x = 20$$

That's J.

17. D

Remember to check for opportunities to simplify fractions before multiplying or dividing with them. Doing so gives you smaller numbers to calculate, which can save you a lot of extra work. In $\frac{3}{7} \times \frac{4}{3}$, the 3 in the numerator of the left fraction and the 3 in the denominator of the right fraction can be cancelled out, reducing the problem to $\frac{1}{7} \times \frac{4}{1} = \frac{4}{7}$. That's D.

Chapter Six: **Elementary Algebra Practice**

PRACTICE QUESTIONS

1. What is 6% of 1250?

   A. 75
   B. 208
   C. 300
   D. 750

2. On her first three geometry tests, Sarah scored an 89, a 93, and an 84. If there are four tests total and Sarah needs at least a 90 average for the four, what is the lowest score she can receive on the final test?

   F. 86
   G. 90
   H. 92
   J. 94

3. The relationship between Fahrenheit and Celsius is $F = \frac{9}{5}C + 32$. If the temperature is 68° Fahrenheit, what is the temperature in degrees Celsius?

   A. 14°
   B. 20°
   C. 32°
   D. 68°

   $68 = \frac{9}{5}C + 32$

   $\left(\frac{5}{9}\right) 36 = \frac{9}{5}C$

4. The eighth grade girls' basketball team played a total of 13 games this season. If they scored a total of 364 points, what was their average score per game?

   F. 13
   G. 16
   H. 20
   J. 28

KAPLAN

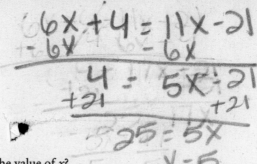

5. If $6x + 4 = 11x - 21$, what is the value of x?

    A. 2
    B. 3
    C. 4
    D. 5

6. A jacket with an original price of $160 is on sale for 15% off. What is the sale price?

    F. $120
    G. $136
    H. $140
    J. $155

7. If the average of 292, 305, 415, and x is 343, what is the value of x?

    A. 315
    B. 337
    C. 360
    D. 382

8. A jar contains 8 red marbles, 14 blue marbles, 11 yellow marbles, and 6 green marbles. If a marble is selected at random, what is the probability that it will be green?

    F. $\dfrac{2}{39}$
    G. $\dfrac{2}{13}$
    H. $\dfrac{8}{39}$
    J. $\dfrac{11}{39}$

9. Each day, Laura bikes to school in the morning and bikes home in the afternoon. If she bikes at a speed of 12 miles per hour and the school is 3 miles from her house, how long does it take her to bike to school and back?

   A. 15 minutes

   B. 24 minutes

   C. 28 minutes

   D. 30 minutes

10. A local high school is raffling off a college scholarship to the students in its junior class. If a girl has a .55 chance of winning the scholarship and 154 of the juniors are girls, how many of the juniors are boys? (Assume that every junior has an equal chance to win.)

    F. 85

    G. 126

    H. 154

    J. 161

    $154 \div .55$

    280

    $280 - 154$

11. At a summer camp, students may choose between a sports elective—basketball, baseball, or soccer—and an exercise elective—yoga or Pilates. The table below shows the number of students enrolled in each elective. If each student enrolled in exactly one elective, what percentage of students enrolled in an exercise elective?

	Elective	Number of Students Enrolled
Sports	Basketball	21
	Baseball	18
	Soccer	13
Exercise	Yoga	13
	Pilates	15

    A. 28%

    B. 35%

    C. 51%

    D. 60%

    $80 = 100\%$

    52

    28

    $\dfrac{28}{80} * 100\% = \dfrac{7}{20} = .35$

KAPLAN

12. During spring break, Robert drove 240 miles to his vacation home. If he drove 60 miles per hour for the first half of the trip and 40 miles per hour for the remaining half, what was his average speed, in miles per hour, for the duration of his trip?

    F. 40
    G. 44
    H. 46
    J. 48

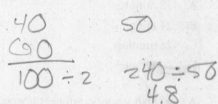

13. In a science class, the midterm is worth 30%, the final exam is worth 50%, and a class project is worth 20%. If Jason scored 86% on the midterm, 95% on the final, and 89% on the project, what was his final grade in the class, rounded to the nearest integer?

    A. 90
    B. 91
    C. 92
    D. 93

$$86+86+86+95+95+95+95+95+$$
$$89+89$$
$$911/10$$
$$91.1$$

14. The expression $3x^2y(xy^2 + 4x^3y)$ is equivalent to

    F. $3xy + 12x$
    G. $xy^2 + 4x^3y$
    H. $15x^8y^5$
    J. $3x^3y^3 + 12x^5y^2$

15. What is the sum of the prime factors of 60?

    A. 12
    B. 16
    C. 19
    D. 24

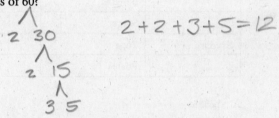

$$2+2+3+5=12$$

16. What is the value of the ones digit in the solution to 2^{326}?

    F. 0
    G. 2
    H. 4
    J. 6

17. The normal price for a pair of skis is $399. If the skis are 10% off and the shop charges 8.75% sales tax, what is the total sale price of the skis?

    A. $359.10
    B. $390.52
    C. $394.01
    D. $433.91

39.9

399 − 39.9

359.1 × 8.75

.0125%

ANSWERS AND EXPLANATIONS

1. A

The quickest way to solve this problem is to estimate. While you may or may not know 6% of 1250 off the top of your head, 10% of 1250 is 125. Since 6% < 10%, the correct answer must be less than 125. Only A works.

To solve this the math way, multiply 1250 by the decimal form of 6%: $1250 \times .06 = 75$.

2. J

When an average problem involves variables, it often helps to think in terms of sum instead. For Sarah's exam scores to average at least a 90, they must sum to at least $90 \times 4 = 360$. She already has an 89, a 93, and an 84, so she needs at least $360 - (89 + 93 + 84) = 360 - 266 = 94$ points on her last test. J is correct.

3. B

You are given the equation to convert Fahrenheit to Celsius, so plug 68 in for F and solve for C:

$$F = \frac{9}{5}C + 32$$

$$68 = \frac{9}{5}C + 32$$

$$36 = \frac{9}{5}C$$

$$20 = c$$

This matches B.

4. J

The basketball team scored 364 points in 13 games, so they scored an average of $\frac{364}{13} = 28$ points per game. Choice J is correct.

5. D

Isolate the variable, then solve for x:

$$6x + 4 = 11x - 21$$
$$4 = 5x - 21$$
$$25 = 5x$$
$$5 = x$$

That's D.

6. G

The original price of the jacket is $160, so a 15% sale is a discount of $160 \times .15 = 24. Therefore, the sale price of the jacket is $160 - $24 = $136. This matches G.

7. C

If the variable makes the average seem difficult to calculate, consider the sum instead. The average of four numbers is 343, so their sum must be $343 \times 4 = 1372$. Three of the numbers are 292, 305, and 415, so the final number is $1372 - (292 + 305 + 415) = 1372 - 1012 = 360$, or C.

8. G

The probability of an event occurring is given by the formula:

$$\text{Probability} = \frac{\text{number of desired outcomes}}{\text{number of possible outcomes}}$$

In this problem, a desired outcome is getting a green marble while a possible outcome is simply getting any marble. There are $8 + 14 + 11 + 6 = 39$ total marbles in the jar. Of these, six are green, so the probability of getting a green marble is $\frac{6}{39}$, which simplifies to $\frac{2}{13}$. That's choice G.

9. D

Laura lives three miles from school, so biking to school and back means a total distance of $3 \times 2 = 6$ miles. Since Laura bikes at a speed of 12 miles per hour and 6 is half of 12, it must take her half an hour, or 30 minutes, to bike both legs of the journey. D is correct.

10. G

There's a lot going on in this problem so find the most concrete point and begin there. You are told that the chance for a girl to win the scholarship is .55. Since this is more than half, there must be more girls than boys in the junior class, so eliminate H and J. .55 isn't much greater than .5, so if you were low on time on Test Day, G would be a great guess.

To solve this problem the math way, use the probability formula:

$$\text{Probability} = \frac{\text{number of desired outcomes}}{\text{number of possible outcomes}}$$

Since .55 is the probability that a girl would win, the 154 girls are the desired outcomes, and the total number of students (boys and girls) is the number of possible outcomes. Call x this total and use this formula to solve for x:

$$.55 = \frac{154}{x}$$
$$x = \frac{154}{.55}$$
$$x = 280$$

With 280 total students and 154 girls, there must be $280 - 154 = 126$ boys. That's G.

11. B

There are a total of $21 + 18 + 13 + 13 + 15 = 80$ students at the camp. Of these, 13 are taking yoga and 15 are taking Pilates, for a total of $13 + 15 = 28$ students taking an exercise elective. Therefore, $\frac{28}{80}$ of the students are taking an exercise elective, which corresponds to $\frac{28}{80} \times 100\% = \frac{7}{20} \times 100\% = 35\%$. B is correct.

12. J

On Test Day, the correct answer to an average speed problem will **never** be the average of the two speeds. To find Robert's average speed, use the following formula:

$$\text{Average} = \frac{\text{total distance}}{\text{total time}}$$

You are given the total distance of 240 miles but you will need to determine the total time. Robert drove the first 120 miles at 60 miles per hour, so it took him $\frac{120}{60} = 2$ hours to do so. He then drove the other 120 miles at 40 miles per hour, so that portion took him $\frac{120}{40} = 3$ hours. Hence, it took him a total of $2 + 3 = 5$ hours to drive all 240 miles, for an average speed of $\frac{240}{5} = 48$ miles per hour. J is correct.

13. B

This average problem contains weighted terms, so you cannot simply use the normal average formula to solve it. There are many ways to tackle this kind of problem but, since all the weights are multiples of 10%, the easiest way is to simply add an instance of each grade for every 10% of weight it carries.

The midterm is worth 30% of Jason's grade, so the 86% it scored counts three times.

The final is worth 50% of Jason's grade, so the 95% it carries counts five times.

The class project is worth 20% of his grade, so the 89% he received counts twice.

This gives Jason a sum of $86 + 86 + 86 + 95 + 95 + 95 + 95 + 95 + 89 + 89 = 911$. There are 10 terms, so the average is $\frac{911}{10} = 91.1$, which is closest to B.

14. J

To multiply exponential terms with the same base, add the exponents. Simplify the expression by distributing the $3x^2y$:

$$3x^2y(xy^2 + 4x^3y) = (3x^2y \times xy^2) + (3x^2y \times 4x^3y) = 3x^3y^3 + 12x^5y^2$$

That looks like J.

15. A

To find the prime factors of 60, use the prime factorization tree:

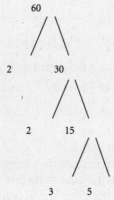

So the prime factorization of 60 is $2 \times 2 \times 3 \times 5$ and the sum of these factors is $2 + 2 + 3 + 5 = 12$.

A is correct.

16. H

2^{326} cannot be evaluated on your calculator, but fortunately, we only need the value of the ones digit. To find it, let's examine the powers of 2 for a pattern:

$2^1 = 2$	$2^5 = 32$
$2^2 = 4$	$2^6 = 64$
$2^3 = 8$	$2^7 = 128$
$2^4 = 16$	$2^8 = 256$

As you can see, the ones digit repeats every four terms. According to this pattern, every exponent with a multiple of 4 will have a ones digit of 6. The largest multiple of 4 that's less than 326 is 324, so 2^{324} will have a ones digit of 6. Therefore, 2^{325} will have a ones digit of 2 and 2^{326} will have a ones digit of 4. This makes H the correct choice.

17. B

This problem requires a couple of steps, so take them one at a time. The skis are discounted 10%, so the pretax price is $399 \times .9 = \$359.10$. This sale price receives an 8.75% tax, so the total sale price is $\$359.10 \times 1.0875 = \$390.52$. B is correct.

Chapter Seven: Intermediate Algebra Practice

PRACTICE QUESTIONS

1. For all x, $(x + 4)(x - 4) + (2x + 2)(x - 2) = ?$
    A. $x^2 - 2x - 20$
    B. $3x^2 - 12$
    C. $3x^2 - 2x - 20$
    D. $3x^2 + 2x - 20$

    $(x^2 - 4x + 4x - 12) + (2x^2 - 2x + 2x - 4)$
    $(x^2 - 12) + (2x^2 - 4)$
    $3x^2 - 16$

2. If $s^2 - 4s - 6 = 6$, what are the possible values of s?
    F. $-2, -6$
    G. $-2, 6$
    H. $2, -6$
    J. $2, 6$

    $s^2 - 4s - 12 = 0$
    $(s + 2)(s - 6)$
    $s^2 - 6s + 2s - 12$

3. In a high school senior class, the ratio of girls to boys is 5:3. If there are a total of 168 students in the senior class, how many girls are there?
    A. 63
    B. 100
    C. 105
    D. 147

    $5 : (3 + 5)$
    $\dfrac{5}{8} = \dfrac{x}{168}$
    $8x = 840$
    $x = 105$

4. If a car drives 80 miles per hour for x hours and 60 miles per hour for y hours, what is the car's average speed, in miles, for the total distance traveled?

F. $\dfrac{480}{xy}$

G. $\dfrac{80}{x}+\dfrac{60}{y}$

H. $\dfrac{80}{x}\times\dfrac{60}{y}$

J. $\dfrac{80x+60y}{x+y}$

5. If the first and second terms of a geometric sequence are 3 and 12, what is the expression for the value of the 24th term of the sequence?

A. $a_{24}=3^4\times 12$

B. $a_{24}=3^4\times 23$

C. $a_{24}=4^3\times 12$

D. $a_{24}=4^{23}\times 3$

6. If $3^{3x+3}=27^{\left(\frac{2}{3}x-\frac{1}{3}\right)}$, then $x=?$

F. -4

G. $-\dfrac{7}{4}$

H. $-\dfrac{10}{7}$

J. 2

$$\left(3x+3\right)=\tfrac{2}{3}x-\tfrac{1}{3}\left(27\right)$$

$$3^{3x+3}=3^{3\left(\frac{2}{3}x-\frac{1}{3}\right)}$$

$$3x+3=2x-1$$

$$x=-4$$

7. The complex number i is defined as $i^2=-1$. $(i+1)^2(i-1)=$

A. $i-1$

B. $i-2$

C. $-2i+2$

D. $-2i-2$

$$(i+1)(i+1)$$

$$(i^2+1i+1i+1)$$

$$(-1+2i+1)(i-1)$$

$$(2i)(i-1)$$

$$2i^2-2i$$

$$2(-1)-2i$$

$$-2-2i$$

8. A playground is $(x + 7)$ units long and $(x + 3)$ units wide. If a square of side length x is sectioned off from the playground to make a sandpit, which of the following could be the remaining area of the playground?

   F. $x^2 + 10x + 21$
   G. $10x + 21$
   H. $2x + 10$
   J. 21

   $(x+7)$

   $(x+3)$

   $(x+7)(x+3)$ $x^2 +10x+21$
   $x^2 +3x +7x +21$

9. If u is an integer, then $(u - 3)^2 + 5$ must be

   A. an even integer
   B. an odd integer
   C. a positive integer
   D. a negative integer

   $(u-3)(u-3)$

   $u^2 -3u -3u +9$

   $u^2 -9u +4$

10. An international phone call costs x cents for the first 5 minutes and t cents for each minute after. What is the cost, in cents, of a call lasting exactly v minutes where $v > 5$?

    F. $\dfrac{5x + t}{v}$
    G. $(5x + t)v$
    H. $5x + tv$
    J. $x + t(v - 5)$

11. Which of the following is a solution for the inequality $|x - 3| + 6 < 15$?

    A. $-6 < x < 12$
    B. $-9 < x < 9$
    C. $x < -9$
    D. $x < -6$

12. In one afternoon, Brian sold 25% of his chocolate bars. If he had 72 bars left, how many chocolate bars did he have to begin with?

    F. 24
    G. 47
    H. 90
    J. 96

13. What is the median of the following list of numbers: 3, 8, 5, 13, 9, 15, 3?

    A. 3
    B. 8
    C. 9
    D. 13

14. What is the value of x in the system of equations below?

$$3y + 4x = 10$$
$$2y - 4x = 0$$

    F. −1
    G. 0
    H. 1
    J. 2

15. A jar contains 15 red marbles, 10 green marbles, and 11 blue marbles. What is the probability that a marble chosen at random from the jar will not be green?

    A. $\dfrac{5}{18}$
    B. $\dfrac{5}{12}$
    C. $\dfrac{7}{12}$
    D. $\dfrac{13}{18}$

16. As museum souvenirs, each of 50 students had the option of buying either mugs or dinosaurs. If 37 bought mugs, 28 bought dinosaurs, and every student bought at least one souvenir, how many students bought both mugs and dinosaurs?

    F. 11
    G. 12
    H. 13
    J. 15

17. If $x^2 - 11x + 24 = 0$, which of the following is a possible solution for x?

    A. -8

    B. -6

    C. -3

    D. 3

$$9 - 33 + 24 = 0$$

ANSWERS AND EXPLANATIONS

1. C

This problem seems long but it actually isn't that complicated. The order of operations says that all of the multiplication should be taken care of first. Let's begin with the first two terms:

$$(x + 4)(x - 4)$$

(If you noticed the difference of squares here, that will save you some time. If not, use FOIL.)

First: $x \times x = x^2$ Outer: $x \times -4 = -4x$
Inner: $4 \times x = 4x$ Last: $4 \times -4 = -16$
Combine like terms: $x^2 + (-4x) + 4x + (-16) = x^2 - 16$

Now for the other two terms:

$$(2x + 2)(x - 2)$$

First: $2x \times x = 2x^2$ Outer: $2x \times -2 = -4x$
Inner: $2 \times x = 2x$ Last: $2 \times -2 = -4$
Combine like terms: $2x^2 + (-4x) + 2x + (-4) = 2x^2 - 2x - 4$

Finally, add the two polynomials: $(x^2 - 16) +$
$(2x^2 - 2x - 4) = 3x^2 - 2x - 20$

That looks like C.

2. G

To solve a quadratic equation, first set it equal to 0. Begin by subtracting 6 from both sides of the equation to get $s^2 - 4s - 12 = 0$. To factor this, you will need two factors of -12 that add up to -4. The only pair of factors that meets this criterion is -6 and 2, so the equation factors to $(s + 2)(s - 6) = 0$. For this equation to be true, either $s + 2$ or $s - 6$ (or both) must be 0. Therefore, the two possible solutions of s are -2 and 6. G is correct.

3. C

The ratio of girls to boys is 5:3 so the ratio of girls to the total number of seniors is 5:(3 + 5) or 5:8. Call x the number of girls in the senior class. Set up the proportion and solve for x:

$$\frac{5}{8} = \frac{x}{168}$$
$$8x = 840$$
$$x = 105$$

There are 105 girls in the senior class, which is C.

4. J

With variables in the question stem and the answer choices, this problem is perfect for picking numbers. Pick 2 for x and 3 for y. Now the problem reads: "If a car drives 80 miles per hour for 2 hours and 60 miles per hour for 3 hours, what is the car's average speed, in miles, for the total distance traveled?"

In this case, the car would have driven $80 \times 2 = 160$ miles and $60 \times 3 = 180$ miles, for a total of $160 + 180 = 340$ miles in five hours. The average speed is therefore $\frac{340}{5} = 68$ miles per hour. Plug 2 in for x and 3 in for y into each of the choices and see which comes out to 68:

F. $\dfrac{480}{2 \times 3} = \dfrac{480}{6} = 80.$ Eliminate.

G. $\dfrac{80}{2} + \dfrac{60}{3} = 40 + 20 = 60.$
Eliminate.

H. $\dfrac{80}{2} \times \dfrac{60}{3} = 40 \times 20 = 800.$
Eliminate.

J. $\dfrac{80(2) + 60(3)}{2 + 3} = \dfrac{160 + 180}{5} = \dfrac{340}{5} = 68.$
This works.

Only J works, so it must be correct.

5. D

In a geometric sequence, use the formula: $a_n = a_1(r^{n-1})$

Where a_n is the nth term in the sequence, a_1 is the first term in the sequence, and r is the amount by which each preceding term is multiplied to get the next term.

The first two terms in this sequence are 3 and 12, so r is $\frac{12}{3} = 4$. Now that we have r, we can plug each known value in the equation and solve for a_{24}:

$$a_{24} = 3(4^{24-1}) = 3 \times 4^{23}$$

That's D.

6. F

When an exponent equation looks difficult on Test Day, try to rewrite the problem so that either the bases or the exponents themselves are the same. In this problem, the two bases seem different at first glance but, since 27 is actually 3^3, you can rewrite the equation as

$$3^{3x+3} = 3^{3\left(\frac{2}{3}x - \frac{1}{3}\right)}$$

This simplifies to $3^{3x+3} = 3^{2x-1}$. Now that the bases are equal, set the exponents equal to each other and solve for x:

$$3x + 3 = 2x - 1$$
$$x + 3 = -1$$
$$x = -4$$

That's F.

7. D

A complex number can seem scary on the ACT but this problem defines it for you, so treat it like you would any other variable that you plug numbers into. In this problem, the key is swapping every i^2 with a −1. Begin by simplifying the first term in the expression:

$$(i + 1)^2 = (i + 1)(i + 1) = i^2 + 2i + 1$$
$$= -1 + 2i + 1 = 2i$$

Multiplying this by the second term gets you
$$2i(i - 1) = 2i^2 - 2i = 2(-1) - 2i = -2 - 2i$$

That's the same as D.

8. G

This is an area problem with a twist—we're cutting a piece out of the rectangle. To find the area of the remaining space, you will need to subtract the area of the sandpit from the area of the original playground. Recall that the area of a rectangle is length × width. The dimensions of the original playground are $x + 7$ and $x + 3$, so its area is $(x + 7)(x + 3) = x^2 + 10x + 21$. The sandpit is a square with side x, so its area is x^2. Remove the pit from our playground and the remaining area is $x^2 + 10x + 21 - x^2 = 10x + 21$. G is correct.

9. C

When a problem tests a number property, the easiest way to solve it is to pick numbers. Since u is an integer, let's pick some integers for u. If $u = 2$, then $(u - 3)^2 + 5 = (2 - 3)^2 + 5 = (-1)^2 + 5 = 1 + 5 = 6$. This eliminates B, D, and E. If $u = 3$, then $(u - 3)^2 + 5 = (3 - 3)^2 + 5 = 5$. This eliminates A, leaving C as the correct answer.

10. J

With so many variables in both the question stem and the answer choices, this problem is ripe for picking numbers. Pick 10 for x, 3 for t, and 9 for v. Now the problem reads, "An international phone call costs 10 cents for the first 5 minutes and 3 cents for each minute after. What is the cost, in cents, of a call lasting exactly 9 minutes?"

In this case, the first 5 minutes costs 10 cents and there are $9 - 5 = 4$ additional minutes, each of which costs 3 cents, for a total cost of $10 + (4 \times 3) = 10 + 12 = 22$ cents. Plug 10 for x, 3 for t, and 9 for v into each of the choices to see which comes out to 22:

F. $\frac{5(10) + 3}{9} = \frac{53}{9} = 5\frac{8}{9}$. Eliminate.

G. $(5(10) + 3)(9) = (50 + 3)(9) = (53)(9) = 477$. Eliminate.

H. $(5 \times 10) + (3 \times 9) = 50 \times 27 = 1350$. Eliminate.

J. $10 + 3(9 - 5) = 10 + 3(4) = 10 + 12 = 22$. This works.

Only J works, so it must be correct.

11. A

The absolute value of a number is its positive distance from 0 on the number line. In other words, the absolute value of a number, much like counting numbers, can never be negative. To solve this problem, begin by isolating the absolute value term on one side:

$$|x - 3| + 6 < 15$$
$$|x - 3| < 9$$

This means that $|x - 3|$ lies somewhere between -9 and 9 on the number line, which can be written as $-9 < x - 3 < 9$. Adding 3 to all parts of the inequality then yields $-6 < x < 12$. That's A.

12. J

With numbers in the answer choices, this problem is an excellent candidate to backsolve. Brian is left with 72 bars *after* selling 25% of his original stock, so he must have started with *more* than 72 bars. Eliminate F and G. Backsolve the remaining three choices. Begin in the middle with J:

Starting with 96 bars and selling 25% leaves him with $96 - .25(96) = 96 - 24 = 72$. That works.

13. B

The median of a set of numbers with an odd number of terms is the middle number. However, this only applies to a set of numbers in numerical order. To find the median of this set, first rewrite the numbers in numerical order: 3, 3, 5, 8, 9, 13, 15.

The middle term is 8, so the answer is B.

14. H

To solve for a variable in a system of equations, you need as many *distinct* equations as you have variables. In this problem, we have two variables, x and y, and two distinct equations. To solve for x, we can either use combination or substitution. Let's have a look at combination:

$$
\begin{array}{r}
3y + 4x = 10 \\
+ (2y - 4x = 0) \\
\hline
5y = 10 \\
y = 2
\end{array}
$$

Plugging 2 in for y into the second equation yields:

$$2y - 4x = 0$$
$$2(2) - 4x = 0$$
$$4 - 4x = 0$$
$$4x = 4$$
$$x = 1$$

For substitution, solve for y in terms of x in one of the equations:

$$2y - 4x = 0$$
$$2y = 4x$$
$$y = 2x$$

Now plug $2x$ in for y into the other equation:

$$3y + 4x = 10$$
$$3(2x) + 4x = 10$$
$$6x + 4x = 10$$
$$10x = 10$$
$$x = 1$$

In either case, $x = 1$, which is choice H.

15. D

The probability of an event occurring is given by the formula:

$$\text{Probability} = \frac{\text{number of desired outcomes}}{\text{number of possible outcomes}}$$

In this problem, a desired outcome is getting a marble that isn't green while a possible outcome is simply getting any marble. There are $15 + 10 + 11 = 36$ total marbles in the jar. Of these, $15 + 11 = 26$ aren't green, so the probability of getting a nongreen marble is $\frac{26}{36}$, which simplifies to $\frac{13}{18}$. That's choice D.

16. J

In this problem, some of the students bought mugs, some bought dinosaurs, and some bought both. The problem is asking for the number of students who bought both. Thirty-seven bought mugs and 28 bought dinosaurs, which accounts for a total of $37 + 28 = 65$ students. Since there are only 50 students in total, $65 - 50 = 15$ students were counted twice. These 15 are the ones who bought both mugs and dinosaurs. That's J.

17. D

If you aren't comfortable with factoring quadratics, a bit of critical thinking can be all you need to solve this problem. Since "$x^2 + 24$" is positive, the only way for the equation to equal 0 is for the middle term, $-11x$, to be negative—that is, x *needs* to be positive. Eliminate A, B, and C. Backsolve the remaining two choices to find the answer. Try D first.

D. $x^2 - 11x + 24 = (3)^2 - 11(3) + 24 = 9 - 33 + 24 = 0$.

This works, so it must be correct.

Chapter Eight: **Coordinate Geometry Practice**

PRACTICE QUESTIONS

1. Which of the following is a solution to the inequality $-1 \geq -\dfrac{3}{5}x + 2$?

    A.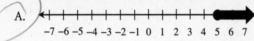

    -7 -6 -5 -4 -3 -2 -1 0 1 2 3 4 5 6 7

    B. ←—+—+—+—+—+—+—+—+—+—+—+—+—○———▶

    -7 -6 -5 -4 -3 -2 -1 0 1 2 3 4 5 6 7

    C. ◀———————————————————●—+—+—▶

    -7 -6 -5 -4 -3 -2 -1 0 1 2 3 4 5 6 7

    D. ◀———————————————————○—+—▶

    -7 -6 -5 -4 -3 -2 -1 0 1 2 3 4 5 6 7

2. If $f(x) = \dfrac{1}{3}x + 13$ and $g(x) = 3x^2 + 6x + 12$, what is the value of $f(g(x))$?

    F. $x^2 + 12x + 4$

    G. $\dfrac{x^2}{3} + 2x + 194$

    H. $x^2 + 2x + 17$

    J. $x^2 + 2x + 25$

$\frac{1}{3}(3x^2 + 6x + 12) + 13$

$x^2 + 2x + 4 + 13$

$x^2 + 2x + 17$

3. What is the length of side AC in triangle ABC graphed on the coordinate plane below?

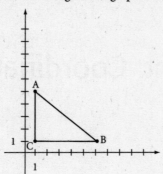

A. 3
B. 4
C. 5
D. 6

4. If $f(x) = 3\sqrt{x^2 + 3x + 4}$, what is the value of $f(4)$?

F. 4
G. $3\sqrt{2}$
H. $4\sqrt{2}$
J. $12\sqrt{2}$

$3\sqrt{4^2 + 3(4) + 4}$

$3\sqrt{16 + 12 + 4}$

$f(4) = 3\sqrt{32}$

$4f = 3\sqrt{32}$

$3 \times 4\sqrt{2}$

5. What is the equation of a line that is perpendicular to the line $y = \dfrac{2}{3}x + 5$ and contains the point $(4, -3)$?

A. $y = \dfrac{2}{3}x + 4$

B. $y = -\dfrac{2}{3}x + 3$

C. $y = -\dfrac{3}{2}x + 3$

D. $y = -\dfrac{3}{2}x - 9$

6. Which of the following is the equation of the graph below?

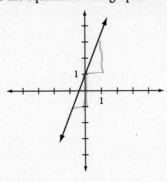

F. $y = 2x + 1$
G. $y = -2x + 1$
H. $y = \dfrac{1}{2}x + 1$
J. $y = -\dfrac{1}{2}x + 1$

0, 1
1, 3

$\dfrac{3-1}{1-0}$ $\dfrac{2}{1}$ 2

7. In the figure below, at which point does $\overline{XZ}$ intersect with its perpendicular bisector?

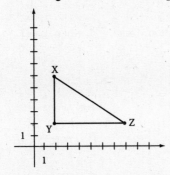

A. (4, 5)
B. (2, 4)
C. (5, 2)
D. (5, 4)

$\dfrac{2 \quad 8}{x^1 + x^2}{2}$ $\dfrac{6 \quad 2}{y^1 + y^2}{2}$

$\dfrac{2+8}{2}$ $\dfrac{6+2}{2}$

$\dfrac{10}{2}$ 5 $\dfrac{8}{2}$ 4

8. What is the length of a line segment with endpoints (3, −6) and (−2, 6)?

F. 1
G. 5
H. 10
J. 13

$\sqrt{(-2-3)^2 + (6-(-6))^2}$

$\sqrt{25 + 144}$

$\sqrt{169}$

9. What is the midpoint of the line segment in the graph below?

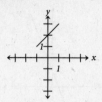

   A. (0, 1)

   B. (0, 2)

   C. (1, 2)

   D. (1, 1)

$-1, 1 \qquad 1, 3$

$\dfrac{-1+1}{2} \qquad \dfrac{1+3}{2}$

$0 \qquad 2$

10. What is the x-intercept of the line described by $3x + y = 9$?

   F. 1

   G. 2

   H. 3

   J. 6

$3x + 0 = 9$

$3x = 9$

$x = 3$

11. Which of the following could be a graph of the equation $y = ax^2 - 4$, when $a > 1$?

   A.

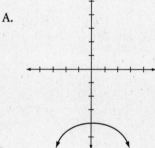

   B.

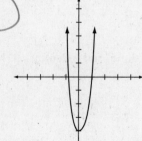

C.

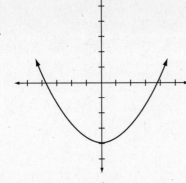

D.

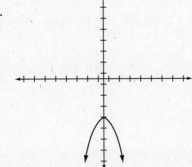

12. What is the equation of a line that has a y-intercept of -3 and is parallel to the line $3x = 4 + 5y$?

A. $y = -\dfrac{3}{5}x + 3$

B. $y = -\dfrac{5}{3}x - 3$

C. $y = \dfrac{3}{5}x + 3$

D. $y = \dfrac{3}{5}x - 3$

$3x = 4 + 5(-3)$

$3x = 4 - 15$

$3x = -11$

13. What is the area of the figure below?

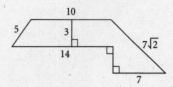

    A. $39 + 7\sqrt{2}$
    B. 60.5
    C. 91
    D. 108.5

14. Which of the following represents the equation of the biggest circle that could fit inside an ellipse with the following equation:

$$\frac{(x-4)^2}{16} + \frac{(y+3)^2}{25} = 1$$

    F. $(x-4)^2 + (y+3)^2 = 400$
    G. $(x-4)^2 + (y+3)^2 = 25$
    H. $(x-4)^2 + (y+3)^2 = 16$
    J. $x^2 + (y+3)^2 = 25$

15. What is the equation of a line that passes through the origin and is perpendicular to the line $2y = 4x - 6y + 4$?

    A. $y = \frac{1}{2}x + \frac{1}{2}$

    B. $y = \frac{1}{2}x$

    C. $y = 2x$

    D. $y = -2x$

16. What is the length of an arc with a central angle of 60° in a circle of radius 6?

    F. 2π
    G. 4π
    H. 6π
    J. 12π

17. What is the value of $f(g(3))$ if $f(x) = 2x - 4$ and $g(x) = 3x^2 - 2$?

    A. 25
    B. 26
    C. 40
    D. 46

$2((3(3))^2 - 2) - 4$

$2(27 - 2) - 4$

$2(25) - 4$

$50 - 4$

46

ANSWERS AND EXPLANATIONS

1. A

Ignore the number lines for now and focus on the inequality. Inequalities work like normal equations in all aspects except one—when multiplying or dividing by a negative number, remember to flip the inequality sign. To solve this inequality, isolate x:

$$-1 \geq -\frac{3}{5}x + 2$$

$$-3 \geq -\frac{3}{5}x$$

$$5 \leq x$$

"Greater than or equal to 5" is represented by a closed circle at 5 with the arrow pointing toward the right. That's A.

2. H

With nested functions, work from the inside out. To solve this problem, substitute the entire function of $g(x)$ for x in the function $f(x)$, then solve:

$$f(g(x)) = \frac{1}{3}(3x^2 + 6x + 12) + 13$$

$$f(g(x)) = x^2 + 2x + 4 + 13$$

$$f(g(x)) = x^2 + 2x + 17$$

Choice H is correct.

3. B

To find the length of a line segment on the coordinate plane, you would normally need to use the distance formula. This requires the coordinates of the segment's two endpoints. Since A $(1, 5)$ and C $(1, 1)$ have the same x-coordinate, a much faster way is to simply subtract the y-coordinate of C from the y-coordinate of A. The length of segment AC is $5 - 1 = 4$. That's B.

4. J

To find $f(4)$, plug 4 for x into the function $f(x)$ and solve:

$$f(x) = 3\sqrt{x^2 + 3x + 4}$$

$$= 3\sqrt{4^2 + 3(4) + 4}$$

$$= 3\sqrt{16 + 12 + 4}$$

$$= 3\sqrt{32}$$

$$= 3 \times 4\sqrt{2}$$

$$= 12\sqrt{2}$$

So the answer is J.

5. C

Perpendicular lines have negative reciprocal slopes. Since the line in the problem has a slope of $\frac{2}{3}$, the line we are looking for must have a slope of $-\frac{3}{2}$. The problem also says that this line contains the point $(4, -3)$. Plugging all of this information into the equation of a line, $y = mx + b$, will allow us to find the final missing piece—the y-intercept:

$$y = mx + b$$

$$-3 = -\frac{3}{2}(4) + b$$

$$-3 = -6 + b$$

$$3 = b$$

With a slope of $-\frac{3}{2}$ and a y-intercept of 3, the line is $y = -\frac{3}{2}x + 3$. That matches C.

6. F

The line crosses the y-axis at (0, 1), so its y-intercept is 1. Eliminate choice E. A quick look at the four remaining choices reveals that each has a different slope, so finding the slope of our line will be enough to answer the question. We already have one point, (0, 1), so pick another point, such as (1, 3), and plug both into the two-point formula for slope:

$$\text{Slope} = \frac{y_2 - y_1}{x_2 - x_1}$$

$$= \frac{3 - 1}{1 - 0}$$

$$= \frac{2}{1}$$

$$= 2$$

The slope is 2 and the y-intercept is 1, so the line is $y = 2x + 1$. That's F.

7. D

Don't let the triangle fool you—its presence is wholly irrelevant as you only need $\overline{XZ}$ itself to answer the question. A bisector of a line segment cuts the segment in half, so it must intersect that segment at its midpoint. Therefore, we are actually looking for the midpoint of $\overline{XZ}$. According to the figure, the coordinates of $\overline{XZ}$ are (2, 6) for X and (8, 2) for Z. Plug these points into the midpoint formula and solve:

$$\text{Midpoint} = \left(\frac{x_1 + x_2}{2}, \frac{y_1 + y_2}{2} \right)$$

$$= \left(\frac{2 + 8}{2}, \frac{6 + 2}{2} \right)$$

$$= \left(\frac{10}{2}, \frac{8}{2} \right)$$

$$= (5, 4)$$

D is correct.

8. J

To find the distance between two points, plug them into the distance formula and evaluate:

$$\text{Distance} = \sqrt{(x_2 - x_1)^2 + (y_2 - y_1)^2}$$

$$= \sqrt{(-2 - 3)^2 + (6 - (-6))^2}$$

$$= \sqrt{(-5)^2 + 12^2}$$

$$= \sqrt{25 + 144}$$

$$= \sqrt{169}$$

$$= 13$$

J is correct.

9. A

Plug the given points into the midpoint formula and solve:

$$\text{Midpoint} = \left(\frac{x_1 + x_2}{2}, \frac{y_1 + y_2}{2} \right)$$

$$= \left(\frac{1 + (-1)}{2}, \frac{3 + 1}{2} \right)$$

$$= \left(\frac{0}{2}, \frac{4}{2} \right)$$

$$= (0, 2)$$

A is correct.

10. H

The x-intercept of a line is the point at which it crosses the y-axis—that is, the value of x when $y = 0$. To find the x-intercept of this line, plug 0 in for y and solve for x:

$$3x + y = 9$$

$$3x + 0 = 9$$

$$3x = 9$$

$$x = 3$$

Therefore, H is correct.

11. B

This problem only *looks* tough. If parabolas seem Greek to you on Test Day, you can always fall back on picking numbers. Since $a > 1$, let's pick 2 for a, 2 for x, and solve for y:

$$y = ax^2 - 4$$

$$y = 2(2)^2 - 4$$

$$y = 2(4) - 4$$

$$y = 8 - 4$$

$$y = 4$$

So (2, 4) is a solution to our parabola. A quick glance at the choices reveals that only B includes this point.

12. J

Begin by converting $3x = 4 + 5y$ into $y = mx + b$ form:

$$3x = 4 + 5y$$

$$3x - 4 = 5y$$

$$\frac{3}{5}x - \frac{4}{5} = y$$

The slope of this line is $\frac{3}{5}$. Parallel lines have the same

slope, so the line we are looking for has a slope of $\frac{3}{5}$ and a y-intercept of -3. That's J.

13. B

To find the total area of this composite figure, you will need to break it down into simpler figures. The figure has been broken down below.

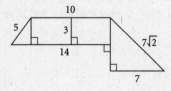

Start with the small right triangle on the left. It has a height of 3 and a hypotenuse of 5, so it must be a 3-4-5 right triangle with a base of 4. Plug these values into the formula to find its area:

$$\text{Area} = \frac{1}{2}bh$$

$$= \frac{1}{2}(4)(3)$$

$$= \frac{1}{2}(12)$$

$$= 6$$

Next, find the area of the large rectangle in the middle. The rectangle has a base of 10 and a height of 3, so plug these values into the formula to find its area:

$$\text{Area} = bh$$

$$= (10)(3)$$

$$= 30$$

Finally, let's deal with the larger right triangle on the right. It has a base of 7 and a hypotenuse of $7\sqrt{2}$, so it must be a 45-45-90 right triangle with a height of 7. Plug these values into the formula to find its area:

$$\text{Area} = \frac{1}{2}bh$$

$$= \frac{1}{2}(7)(7)$$

$$= \frac{1}{2}(49)$$

$$= 24.5$$

To get the total area, sum up the areas of all three pieces: Area = 6 + 30 + 24.5 = 60.5. That's B.

14. H

To solve this problem, you need to know both the equation for an ellipse— $\dfrac{(x-h)^2}{a^2} + \dfrac{(y-k)^2}{b^2} = 1$ —and the equation for a circle— $(x-h)^2 + (y-k)^2 = r^2$. To inscribe the largest possible circle, the circle and ellipse must both be centered at the same point. This eliminates J. Since a circle has a constant radius, the diameter of the largest possible circle inscribed within an ellipse will be equal to the ellipse's shorter axis. In $\dfrac{(x-4)^2}{16} + \dfrac{(y+3)^2}{25}$, $a^2 = 16$ and $b^2 = 25$, so the horizontal ($2a$) and vertical axes ($2b$) are $2 \times 4 = 8$ and $2 \times 5 = 10$, respectively. Since $8 < 10$, our circle has a diameter of 8 and a radius of $\dfrac{8}{2} = 4$. Therefore, $r^2 = 4^2 = 16$, and the equation of the circle is $(x-4)^2 + (y+3)^2 = 16$. H is correct.

15. D

Begin by converting $2y = 4x - 6y + 4$ into $y = mx + b$ form:

$$2y = 4x - 6y + 4$$

$$8y = 4x + 4$$

$$y = \frac{1}{2}x + \frac{1}{2}$$

The slope of this line is $\dfrac{1}{2}$, so a line perpendicular to it that passes through the origin will have a slope of -2 and a y-intercept of 0. That's choice D.

16. F

Plug the given values into the arc length formula and solve:

$$\text{Arc Length} = \frac{\theta}{360} \times 2\pi r$$

$$= \frac{60}{360} \times 2\pi(6)$$

$$= \frac{1}{6} \times 12\pi$$

$$= 2\pi$$

So the arc length is 2π, which is F.

17. D

With nested functions, work from the inside out. Begin by evaluating $g(3)$:

$$g(3) = 3(3)^2 - 2$$

$$= 3(9) - 2$$

$$= 27 - 2$$

$$= 25$$

Now use this value to find $f(g(3))$:

$$f(25) = 2(25) - 4$$

$$= 50 - 4$$

$$= 46$$

D is correct.

Chapter Nine: **Plane Geometry Practice**

PRACTICE QUESTIONS

1. What is the area of a circle with a diameter of 8?

    A. 4π

    B. 8π

    C. 16π

    D. 32π

2. A rectangle has a side length of 8 and a perimeter of 24. What is the area of the rectangle?

    F.   16

    G.   24

    H.   32

    J.   96

Handwritten work:

$2l * 2w$

$24 = 2(8) + 2w$

$24 = 16 + 2w$

$8 = 2w$

$4 = w$

$8 * 4 = 32$

3. Isosceles triangle ABC has an area of 48. If $\overline{AB} = 12$, what is the perimeter of ABC?

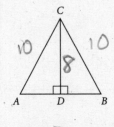

Handwritten work:

$48 = \frac{1}{2}(12)h$

$48 = 6h$

$8 = h$

$(\frac{1}{2})(12)(12)$

    A.   32

    B.   36

    C.   48

    D.   64

4. The rectangular backyard of a house is 130 feet by 70 feet. If the backyard is completely fenced in, what is the length, in feet, of the fence?

    F. 130
    G. 200
    H. 260
    J. 400

5. In the figure below, lines *m* and *l* are parallel and $\angle a = 68°$. What is the measure of $\angle f$?

    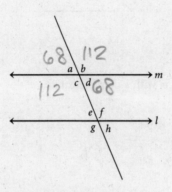

    A. 22°
    B. 68°
    C. 80°
    D. 112°

6. A boy who is 4 ft. tall stands in front of a tree that is 24 ft. tall. If the tree casts a shadow that is 18 ft. long on the ground and the two shadows end at the same point, what is the length of the boy's shadow?

    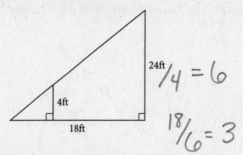

    F. 3 ft.
    G. 4 ft.
    H. 5 ft.
    J. 6 ft.

7. The hypotenuse of right triangle *RST* is 16. If the measure of ∠*R* = 30°, what is the length of *RS*?

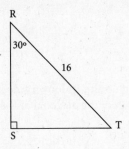

    A. 4
    B. 8
    C. $8\sqrt{3}$
    D. 12

8. Circle *O* has a radius of 5 and ∠*AOB* = 45°. What is the length of arc *AB*?

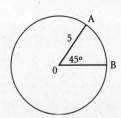

    F. 5
    G. $\dfrac{4\pi}{5}$
    H. 3
    J. $\dfrac{5\pi}{4}$

9. What is the length of the diagonal of a square with sides of length 7?

    A. 7
    B. $7\sqrt{2}$
    C. 14
    D. 21

10. What is the perimeter of a regular hexagon with a side of 11?

    F. 33

    G. 44

    H. 66

    J. 72

11. A rectangle has a perimeter of 28 and its longer side is 2.5 times the length of its shorter side. What is the length of the diagonal of the rectangle, rounded to the nearest tenth?

    A. 4.0

    B. 10.0

    C. 10.8

    D. 12.4

    $$28 = 2x + 2(2.5x)$$
    $$28 = 7x$$
    $$4 = x$$

12. In the figure below, $\overline{MN}$ and $\overline{PQ}$ are parallel. Point A lies on $\overline{MN}$ and points B and C lie on $\overline{PQ}$. If $AB = AC$ and $\angle MAB = 55°$, what is the measure of $\angle ACB$?

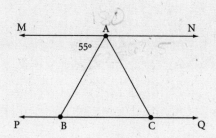

    F. 35°

    G. 55°

    H. 65°

    J. 80°

13. The chord below is 8 units long. If the chord is 3 units from the center of the circle, what is the area of the circle?

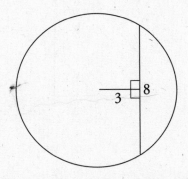

   A. 9π
   B. 16π
   C. 18π
   D. 25π

14. If isosceles triangle *QRS* below has a base of length of 16 and sides of length 17, what is the area of the triangle?

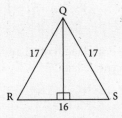

   F. 50
   G. 80
   H. 110
   J. 120

15. Square *QRST* is inscribed inside square *ABCD*. If *QR* = 5, what is the area of triangle *QAT*?

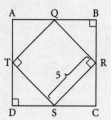

    A. 3

    B. 4.50

    C. 5

    D. 6.25

16. A circle with radius 5 is inscribed in a square. What is the difference between the area of the square and the area of the circle?

    F. 25π

    G. $50 - 25\pi$

    H. $100 - 25\pi$

    J. 100

17. In the figure below, chord *FG* has a length of 12 and triangle *GOH* has an area of 24. What is the area of the circle centered at *O*?

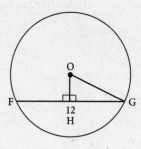

    A. 30π

    B. 36π

    C. 50π

    D. 100π

ANSWERS AND EXPLANATIONS

1. C

A circle with diameter 8 has a radius of $\frac{8}{2}$ = 4. To find the area of this circle, plug this radius into the area formula and solve:

$$\textbf{Area} = \pi r^2$$
$$= \pi(4)^2$$
$$= 16\pi$$

Choice C is correct.

2. H

The perimeter of a rectangle is twice its length plus twice its width, or Perimeter = $2l + 2w$. To find the area, you must first determine the value of w, so plug in the values for perimeter and length to solve:

$$\textbf{Perimeter} = 2l + 2w$$
$$24 = 2(8) + 2w$$
$$24 = 16 + 2w$$
$$8 = 2w$$
$$4 = w$$

So the width is 4. The area of the rectangle is length × width, or 8 × 4 = 32. That's H.

3. A

With only one known side, you cannot find the area directly as you will need to figure out more sides first. Given the area of triangle ABC and its base, the first step is to find height $\overline{CD}$:

$$\textbf{Area} = \frac{1}{2}bh$$
$$48 = \frac{1}{2}(12)h$$
$$48 = 6h$$
$$8 = h$$

So $\overline{CD}$ = 8. Triangle ABC is an isosceles triangle, so $\overline{CD}$ also happens to be the perpendicular bisector of $\overline{AB}$, meaning $\overline{AD} = \overline{DB} = 6$. With legs of 6 and 8, each of the smaller right triangles must be 3-4-5 right triangles, making the hypotenuse of each— $\overline{AC}$ and $\overline{CB}$—10. Therefore, the perimeter of triangle ABC is 10 + 10 + 12 = 32. A is correct.

4. J

It may sound a bit more complex, but this problem is only asking you for the perimeter of a rectangle with the given dimensions so plug them into the perimeter formula and solve:

$$\textbf{Perimeter} = 2l + 2w$$
$$= 2(130) + 2(70)$$
$$= 260 + 140$$
$$= 400$$

J is correct.

5. D

When two parallel lines are cut by a transversal, half of the angles will be acute and half will be obtuse. Each acute angle will have the same measure as each other acute angle. The same is true of every obtuse angle. Furthermore, the acute angles will be supplementary to the obtuse angles. $\angle a$ is an acute angle measuring 68° while $\angle f$ is an obtuse angle, so $\angle a$ must be supplementary to $\angle f$. Therefore, $\angle f = 180° - 68° = 112°$.

That's D.

6. F

While this problem may *look* like a geometry problem at first glance, a closer look reveals that each of the three angles of one triangle is congruent to its corresponding angle in the other. The triangles are thus similar and similar triangles have proportional sides, so this is actually a proportion problem. The boy's height is proportional to the tree's height in the same way that the boy's shadow is proportional to that of the tree, so call x the length of the boy's shadow, set up the proportion, and solve for x:

$$\frac{24}{18} = \frac{4}{x}$$
$$24x = 72$$
$$x = 3$$

So the boy's shadow is 3 ft. long. That's F.

7. C

You are told that triangle *RST* is a right triangle and that one of its angles is 30°, so *RST* must be a 30-60-90 right triangle, meaning its sides must be in the proportion $x : x\sqrt{3} : 2x$. Hypotenuse *RT* is 16, so *x* must be $\frac{16}{2} = 8$ and *RS* (the longer leg) must be $8\sqrt{3}$. That matches C.

8. J

To find the length of an arc, you will need the measure of the central angle as well as the circumference of the entire circle. In this problem, the central angle is 45° and the circumference of the circle is $2\pi(5) = 10\pi$. Plug these values into the proportion and solve:

$$\frac{\text{central angle}}{360°} = \frac{\text{length of arc}}{\text{circumference}}$$

$$\frac{45°}{360°} = \frac{\text{length of arc}}{2\pi r}$$

$$\frac{1}{8} = \frac{\text{length of arc}}{10\pi}$$

$$8 \times (\text{length of arc}) = 10\pi$$

$$\text{length of arc} = \frac{10\pi}{8}$$

$$= \frac{5\pi}{4}$$

J is correct.

9. B

A square has four right angles and four equal sides. Its diagonal cuts the square into two identical isosceles right triangles. The square in this problem has a side length of 7, so the base and height of each isosceles right triangle is also 7. The sides of an isosceles right triangle are in the proportion $x : x : x\sqrt{2}$, so the length of the diagonal (the hypotenuse of both triangles) is $7\sqrt{2}$. B is correct.

10. H

A regular polygon is equilateral, so a regular hexagon is a hexagon with six equal sides. The regular hexagon in the problem has a side of 11, so its perimeter is $6 \times 11 = 66$.

That's H.

11. C

The perimeter of the rectangle is 28 and one of its sides is 2.5 times the length of the other, so call *x* the shorter side. Our rectangle now has sides of *x* and 2.5*x*. Draw a figure to help visualize this problem.

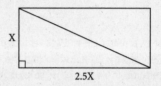

To find *x*, plug the information into the perimeter formula and solve:

$$\textbf{Perimeter} = 2l + 2w$$
$$28 = 2(x) + 2(2.5x)$$
$$28 = 2x + 5x$$
$$28 = 7x$$
$$4 = x$$

So $x = 4$ and the dimensions of the rectangle must be $4 \times 1 = 4$ and $2.5 \times 4 = 10$. These values are not parts of a special right triangle, so use the Pythagorean Theorem to find the diagonal:

$$a^2 + b^2 = c^2$$
$$4^2 + 10^2 = c^2$$
$$16 + 100 = c^2$$
$$116 = c^2$$
$$\sqrt{116} = c$$

Since 116 isn't a perfect square but it lies between $10^2 = 100$ and $11^2 = 121$, $\sqrt{116}$ must be somewhere between 10 and 11. The only choice that fits is C.

12. G

This is a pair of parallel lines cut by a transversal but this time, there's also a triangle thrown into the mix. Begin with $\overline{AB}$. This is a transversal, so $\angle MAB$ and $\angle ABC$ are alternate interior angles and $\angle MAB = \angle ABC = 55°$. Since triangle ABC is isosceles with $AB = AC$, $\angle ACB$ is also 55°.

That's G.

13. D

The chord is perpendicular to the line segment from the center of the circle, so that line segment must be its perpendicular bisector. This allows us to add the following to the figure:

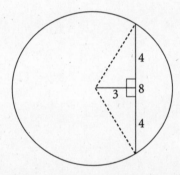

The two right triangles have legs 3 and 4, so they are both 3-4-5 right triangles with hypotenuse 5. This hypotenuse is also the radius of the circle, so plug that into the area formula to solve:

$$\textbf{Area} = \pi r^2$$
$$= \pi(5)^2$$
$$= 25\pi$$

The correct answer is D.

14. J

Triangle QRS is an isosceles triangle so its height is also the perpendicular bisector of $\overline{RS}$. Each half of $\overline{RS}$ is $\frac{16}{2} = 8$ units long, so each of the smaller right triangles has a leg of 8 and a hypotenuse of 17. They must therefore be 8-15-17 right triangles, making the height of QRS 15. Therefore, the area of QRS is $\frac{1}{2} \times 16 \times 15 = \frac{1}{2} \times 240 = 120$. J is correct.

15. D

When a square is inscribed within another square like they are in this problem, each of the inner square's vertices bisects one of the outer square's sides, so point Q bisects $\overline{AB}$ and point T bisects $\overline{AD}$. Therefore, $\overline{QA} = \overline{AT}$ and triangle QAT is an isosceles right triangle. Since $QRST$ is a square and $QR = 5$, RS, ST, and TQ do as well, and triangle QAT becomes an isosceles right triangle with a hypotenuse of 5. An isosceles right triangle has sides in the proportion $x : x : x\sqrt{2}$, so $\overline{QA}$ and $\overline{AT}$ each measure $\frac{5}{\sqrt{2}} = \frac{5\sqrt{2}}{2}$. Plug these into the area formula and solve:

$$Area = \frac{1}{2}bh$$
$$= \frac{1}{2} \times \left(\frac{5\sqrt{2}}{2}\right)^2$$
$$= \frac{1}{2} \times \frac{25 \times 2}{4}$$
$$= \frac{1}{2} \times \frac{50}{4}$$
$$= \frac{50}{8}$$
$$= 6.25$$

That matches D.

16. G

Begin by eliminating A, as $50 - 25\pi$ is a negative value and that cannot be correct. Since the problem does not provide you with a figure, draw one to visualize what you are being asked.

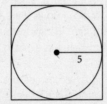

Since the circle is inscribed within the square, its radius is half the side of the square. The circle has a radius of 5, so the square has a side of $2 \times 5 = 10$. Therefore, the area of the circle is $5^2\pi = 25\pi$ and the area of the square is $10^2 = 100$. The difference between the area of the square and that of the circle is thus $100 - 25\pi$. That's G.

17. D

You are given that the area of the triangle inside the circle is 24 and the length of the chord is 12. $\overline{OH}$ comes from the center and is perpendicular to $\overline{FG}$, so the former must be the perpendicular bisector of the latter and $\overline{FH} = \overline{HG} = 6$. Plug this into the area formula to find the length of $\overline{OH}$:

$$\text{Area} = \frac{1}{2}bh$$
$$24 = \frac{1}{2}(6)h$$
$$24 = 3h$$
$$8 = h$$

So $\overline{OH} = 8$, making triangle *HOG* a 3-4-5 right triangle with legs 6 and 8, and a hypotenuse of 10. The latter also happens to be the radius of the circle, so its area is $\pi r^2 = 10^2\pi = 100\pi$. That's D.

Chapter Ten: **Trigonometry Practice**

$$\sin = \frac{OPP}{hyp} \qquad \frac{.6}{15}$$

PRACTICE QUESTIONS

1. In the triangle below, if cos ∠*BAC* = .6 and the hypotenuse of the triangle is 15, what is the length of side *BC*?

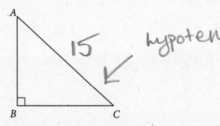

15 ← hypotenus

$$\cos = \frac{adj}{hyp}$$

$$\tan = \frac{opp}{adj}$$

   A. 3
   B. 5
   C. 10
   D. 12

2. What is the tangent of ∠*EFD* below?

5

   F. $\frac{5}{13}$

   G. $\frac{5}{12}$

   H. $\frac{12}{13}$

   J. $\frac{12}{5}$

3. In the triangle below, what is the value of sin ∠QRS?

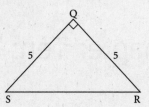

    A. $\dfrac{\sqrt{2}}{6}$

    B. $\dfrac{\sqrt{2}}{5}$

    C. $\dfrac{\sqrt{2}}{2}$

    D. $5\sqrt{2}$

4. In the right triangle below, JL = 17 and KL = 8. What is the value of sin ∠JLK?

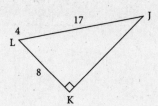

    F. $\dfrac{8}{15}$

    G. $\dfrac{8}{17}$

    H. $\dfrac{8}{20}$

    J. $\dfrac{15}{17}$

5. If $\sin \angle CAB = \dfrac{3}{5}$ and $AC = 15$, what is the value of $\cos \angle CAB$?

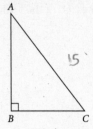

   A. $\dfrac{4}{5}$

   B. 1

   C. $\dfrac{5}{4}$

   D. $\dfrac{15}{4}$

6. The ramp in the figure below has a 20° angle of elevation and a height of 3 ft. What is the length of the ramp?

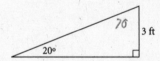

   F. $\dfrac{3}{\sin 20°}$

   G. $\dfrac{3}{\cos 20°}$

   H. $\dfrac{\sin 20°}{3}$

   J. $\dfrac{\cos 20°}{3}$

7. If $\sin A = \dfrac{1}{2}$, which of the following could be the value of $\tan A$?

   A. $\dfrac{\sqrt{3}}{3}$

   B. $\dfrac{1}{3}$

   C. $\dfrac{2}{3}$

   D. $\dfrac{5}{3}$

8.   A building contractor determines that the angle of elevation from the ground to the top of a small office building is 67°. If the contractor is 50 meters from the base of the building, what is the height, in meters, of the building?

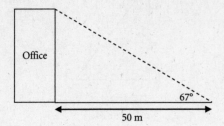

F.   50 sin 67°

G.   50 cos 67°

H.   50 tan 67°

J.   50 cot 67°

9.   In the figure below, which of the following is equivalent to 2?

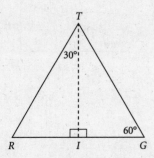

A.   sin ∠TGI

B.   cos ∠RIT

C.   tan ∠RTI

D.   sec ∠TRI

10. If $\tan A = \dfrac{8}{15}$ and $0 \le A \le 90$, which of the following could be a value of $\cos A$?

    F. $\dfrac{8}{17}$

    G. $\dfrac{8}{15}$

    H. $\dfrac{15}{17}$

    J. $\dfrac{17}{15}$

11. In the figure below, all of the following are less than 1 EXCEPT

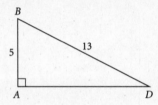

    A. $\sin \angle D$
    B. $\cos \angle D$
    C. $\tan \angle D$
    D. $\csc \angle B$

12. If $\sec \angle A = \dfrac{13}{5}$, which of the following statements must be true?

    F. $\sin \angle A > \cos \angle A$
    G. $\cos \angle A > \tan \angle A$
    H. $\tan \angle A < \cot \angle A$
    J. $\sec \angle A < \csc \angle A$

13. If $0° < \theta < 90°$ and $\cot \theta = \dfrac{4}{5}$, then $\sec \theta = $?

    A. $\dfrac{3}{5}$

    B. $\dfrac{5}{4}$

    C. $\dfrac{5}{3}$

    D. $\dfrac{\sqrt{41}}{4}$

14. George knows that $\angle F$ in the figure below is 65°. Which of the following additional pieces of information would allow him to determine the length of the hypotenuse?

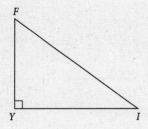

    F. the length of $\overline{YI}$

    G. the value of $\dfrac{\overline{FY}}{\overline{FI}}$

    H. the value of $\dfrac{\overline{YI}}{\overline{FI}}$

    J. the area of triangle FYI

15. In right triangle FAH, $\cot \angle H = 1$. Which of the following must be true?

    A. FAH is a 3-4-5 right triangle

    B. FAH is a 5-12-13 right triangle

    C. FAH is a 45-45-90 right triangle

    D. FAH is a 30-60-90 right triangle

16. If cos G = .5, which of the following would also equal .5?

    F. $1 - \sin G$

    G. $1 - \tan G$

    H. $1\dfrac{1}{-\sin G}$

    J. $1\dfrac{1}{-\sec G}$

17. What is the measure of the angle $\dfrac{3\pi}{4}$ expressed in degrees?

    A.   45°

    B.   60°

    C.   120°

    D.   135°

ANSWERS AND EXPLANATIONS

1. D

You are given the cosine of $\angle BAC$ and the hypotenuse of the triangle, so begin by using these to find the adjacent side:

$$\cos A = \frac{\text{adjacent}}{\text{hypotenuse}}$$

$$.6 = \frac{\text{adjacent}}{15}$$

$$\text{adjacent} = 9$$

So the adjacent side, $\overline{AB}$, is 9 and triangle ABC is a right triangle with a leg of 9 and a hypotenuse of 15. ABC must therefore be a 3-4-5 right triangle and $\overline{BC}$ must be 12. That's D.

2. J

The tangent of an angle is defined by $\tan A = \dfrac{\text{opposite}}{\text{adjacent}}$. The side opposite $\angle EFD$ is 12 and the side adjacent to $\angle EFD$ is 5, so $\tan \angle EFD = \dfrac{12}{5}$. This is J.

3. C

Since $QS = QR$, triangle QRS must be a 45-45-90 right triangle and the hypotenuse is $5\sqrt{2}$. Therefore, $\sin \angle QRS = \dfrac{5}{5\sqrt{2}} = \dfrac{1}{\sqrt{2}} = \dfrac{\sqrt{2}}{2}$. That's choice C.

4. J

A right triangle with leg 8 and hypotenuse 17 must be an 8-15-17 right triangle, so $JK = 15$. Since JK is opposite $\angle JLK$, $\sin \angle JLK = \dfrac{15}{17}$. This matches J.

5. A

You are given the sin of $\angle CAB$ and the hypotenuse of the triangle so begin by using this information to determine the remaining two sides:

$$\sin \angle CAB = \frac{\text{opposite}}{\text{hypotenuse}}$$

$$\frac{3}{5} = \frac{\text{opposite}}{15}$$

$$5 \times \text{opposite} = 45$$

$$\text{opposite} = 9$$

So the opposite side, $\overline{BC}$, is 9 and triangle ABC is a right triangle with a leg of 9 and a hypotenuse of 15. ABC must therefore be a 3-4-5 right triangle and $\overline{AB}$ must be 12. Now use this information to find the cosine of $\angle CAB$:

$$\cos \angle CAB = \frac{\text{adjacent}}{\text{hypotenuse}}$$

$$= \frac{12}{15}$$

$$= \frac{4}{5}$$

So choice A is correct.

6. F

The length of the ramp is the hypotenuse of the right triangle in the figure. Since you only have the side opposite the given angle, use sin 20° to find the hypotenuse:

$$\sin 20° = \frac{\text{opposite}}{\text{hypotenuse}}$$

$$\sin 20° = \frac{3}{\text{hypotenuse}}$$

$$\text{hypotenuse} = \frac{3}{\sin 20°}$$

That's F.

7. A

Drawing a figure can go a long way toward making this problem more concrete. Sin $A = \frac{1}{2}$, so the triangle we are referring to must look like the following:

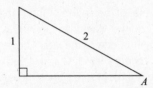

This is a 30-60-90 triangle and its dimensions must be in the proportion $x : x\sqrt{3} : 2x$, so the length of the longer leg is $\sqrt{3}$. Therefore, tan $A = \frac{1}{\sqrt{3}} = \frac{\sqrt{3}}{3}$. Choice A is the correct answer.

8. H

To find the height of the building, you'll need something that gives a relationship between the known angle (67°), the adjacent side (50 meters), and the opposite side (the height of the building we're after). When dealing with opposite and adjacent, tangent should come to mind:

$$\tan 67° = \frac{\text{opposite}}{\text{adjacent}}$$
$$\tan 67° = \frac{\text{height}}{50}$$
$$50 \tan 67° = \text{height}$$

That's choice H.

9. D

The two smaller triangles are 30-60-90 triangles whose sides are in the proportion $x : x\sqrt{3} : 2x$, so pick 1 for x and label the relative lengths of the figure:

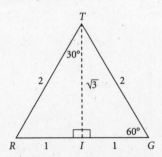

To get a value of 2, we'll need an expression that places the hypotenuse of either of the smaller right triangles over its shorter leg. Of the choices, only D does so it is correct.

10. H

With tan $A = \frac{8}{15}$ and A in the first quadrant, cosine A will also be positive. If you think of this problem as a right triangle with 8 and 15 as the opposite and adjacent legs, respectively, you would have an 8-15-17 right triangle with 17 as the hypotenuse. Therefore, cos A could be $\frac{15}{17}$, which happens to be choice H.

11. D

A right triangle with a leg of 5 and a hypotenuse of 13 is a 5-12-13 right triangle, so the longer leg is 12. Add this information to your figure:

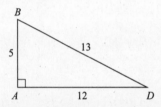

Now, evaluate each choice to find the one that is not less than 1:

A. $\sin \angle D = \frac{\text{opposite}}{\text{hypotenuse}} = \frac{5}{13}$. This is less than 1, so eliminate.

B. $\cos \angle D = \frac{\text{adjacent}}{\text{hypotenuse}} = \frac{12}{13}$. This is less than 1, so eliminate.

C. $\tan \angle D = \frac{\text{opposite}}{\text{adjacent}} = \frac{5}{12}$. This is less than 1, so eliminate.

D. $\csc \angle B = \frac{\text{hypotenuse}}{\text{opposite}} = \frac{13}{12}$. This is greater than 1.

Only D satisfies the criterion, so it must be correct.

12. F

When a figure isn't provided, draw your own.

Sec $\angle A = \dfrac{13}{5}$, so our triangle must be a 5-12-13 triangle like so:

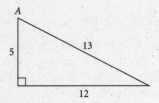

Now, evaluate each choice:

F. $\dfrac{12}{13} > \dfrac{5}{13}$. This works and on Test Day, you would pick it and move on. For the curious:

G. $\dfrac{5}{13} > \dfrac{12}{5}$? Eliminate.

H. $\dfrac{12}{5} < \dfrac{5}{12}$? Eliminate.

J. $\dfrac{13}{5} < \dfrac{13}{12}$? Eliminate.

13. D

This problem can easily be misread so be sure to read the question stem carefully. We are looking for a triangle where **cot** $\theta = \dfrac{4}{5}$. (Had it said **cos** θ, this would be a 3-4-5 right triangle.) Begin by drawing a figure:

Secant involves the hypotenuse, so use the Pythagorean Theorem to find it:

$$a^2 + b^2 = c^2$$
$$4^2 + 5^2 = c^2$$
$$16 + 25 = c^2$$
$$41 = c^2$$
$$\sqrt{41} = c$$

So the hypotenuse is $\sqrt{41}$. Therefore,

$\sec\theta = \dfrac{\text{hypotenuse}}{\text{adjacent}} = \dfrac{\sqrt{41}}{4}$. That's D.

14. F

George knows one of the angles of the triangle and wants to find the hypotenuse. With trigonometry, all he would need is the length of one of the legs. Choice F provides that and is the correct answer. G and H each provide the *ratio* of a leg to the hypotenuse but a ratio alone cannot give us a specific length. J provides information concerning the triangle as a whole but not for one of its sides.

15. C

The cotangent of an angle is $\dfrac{\text{adjacent}}{\text{opposite}}$. In a right triangle, this is a ratio between its two legs. If cot $\angle H = 1$, the length of the adjacent side must equal the length of the opposite side. That only happens in a 45-45-90 right triangle, which is choice C.

16. J

While you may not know the values of most of the choices offhand, you don't need to. Every choice subtracts some value from 1, so the correct answer must subtract an expression that is equal to .5. Since secant is the reciprocal of cosine, $\cos G = \dfrac{1}{\sec G} = .5$, so J is correct.

17. D

To convert $\dfrac{3\pi}{4}$ into degrees, substitute 180 for π and solve:

$$\frac{3\pi}{4} = \frac{3 \times 180}{4}$$
$$= \frac{540}{4}$$
$$= 135°$$

D is correct.

| SECTION THREE |

ACT Science

Chapter Eleven: **Introduction to ACT Science**

The last section of your ACT is Science. The structure of the test is always the same, so you can be certain you'll see seven passages, each with five to seven questions, for a total of 40 questions. You'll have 35 minutes to complete the section. That may not sound like a lot, but don't panic. This guide will show you how to move quickly and find the right answers, and will give you plenty of passages on which to practice your new skills.

The seven passages are drawn from four basic areas of science—biology, chemistry, earth and space sciences, and physics. You'll have one or two passages on each of these topics. Each passage will display data (Data Representation), describe the results of a set of experiments (Research Summaries), or present different views on a single topic (Conflicting Viewpoints). Most passages will include diagrams, charts, or tables with important information.

The purpose of the Science Section is to test your scientific reasoning skills, not your ability to recite specific things you've learned (like the life cycle of a cell). As long as you have a basic understanding of scientific terms and concepts, you won't have to rely on any outside knowledge to answer the questions. What does this mean specifically? It means *the answer is in the passage*. In fact, not only is the answer in the passage, it's printed right below the question. Your only job is to distinguish the correct answer choice from the three incorrect choices it's mixed in with. We've come up with a method to make that easy (we're Kaplan, it's what we do).

THE KAPLAN METHOD FOR ACT SCIENCE

1. **Read the passage, taking notes as you go.**

   Read the introductory paragraph to get an idea of what you're dealing with and quickly read the paragraphs explaining experiment setup. Keep note-taking to a minimum—underline or circle key words (they're often already italicized, which makes your job even easier), and underline or circle specific values (this makes them easier to spot if you need them later). Don't spend more than a minute here.

2. **Skim the figures.**

   Ask yourself two questions: "What does this figure show?" and "What are the units of measurement?" Keep your answers general. Figures usually show how one variable changes with another. Your job at this point is to simply identify what these variables are and what units they're measured in.

3. **Attack the questions.**

   Ask yourself, "Where in the passage can I find the answer to this question?" Quite often, the question stem will point you to just the paragraph or figure you need. Begin with the questions that look easy to you. If you have no idea where to find the answer to a question, save it for last. You'll develop an increasingly clearer understanding of the passage as you answer the questions.

Now let's take a closer look at the three types of passages you'll see on the ACT Science Test: **Data Representation, Research Summaries,** and **Conflicting Viewpoints.**

DATA REPRESENTATION

There are three Data Representation passages on the ACT Science Test, each with five questions.

These passages do just what they say; they show you data. No experiments are conducted, no theories are debated. All that's provided is some information on the page for you to see, mostly in the form of graphs and tables. The questions that correspond with these passages are designed to test your ability to find information in these graphs and tables.

Suppose you saw the following graph in a science passage:

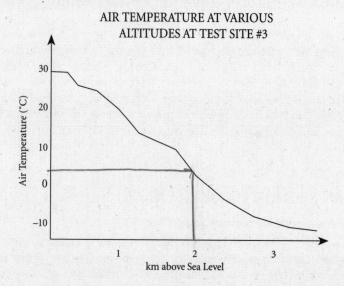

As you're using the Kaplan Method for ACT Science, you'll stop when you reach this figure. You'll say to yourself, "What does this figure show? What are the units of measurement?" Well, the graph shows air temperature at various altitudes at Test Site #3. The temperature is measured in °C (degrees Celsius). Then, you'll just move on! At this point, you don't care what the altitudes are! You don't care what's actually going on in the figure until a *question* asks you. Until it's going to earn you points, it just doesn't matter! Liberating, isn't it?

However, there are going to be questions. Questions like, "What is the temperature at 2 km above Sea Level?" To answer, find 2 km on the *x*-axis (that's the axis on the bottom). Draw a line straight up until you intersect the line. Then, draw a straight line from this point to the *y*-axis (that's the up and down axis). Use your pencil—the graphs are often pretty small, and eyeballing won't always give you an accurate enough estimate. Here, you can see that the temperature at 2 km is about 5°.

Data will also appear in the form of tables. Suppose you came across this in a passage:

| Concentration of *E. coli* in Cooling Pool B ||
DISTANCE FROM EFFLUENT PIPE 3	1000s OF *E. COLI* PER CENTILITRE
zero m	.4
5 m	5.6
10 m	27.6
15 m	14.0
20 m	7.5

Again, you'll identify what the figure shows and the units of measurement (percent doesn't have units, time is in seconds). And again, you'll stop studying the table here. More specific analysis can wait until it'll earn you points.

The questions based on tables will sometimes ask you to identify specific data points. These questions might ask, "Five meters from Effluent Pipe 3, how many thousands of *E. Coli* are found per centiliter of water?" To answer, find 5 in the "Distance" column (that's the row of boxes on the far left, running down). Follow the 5 m row (a row is a line of boxes running horizontally) over to the "1000s of *E. Coli*" column. The value in that box is .4. There are .4 thousands per centiliter.

You might also be asked to identify trends in the data in a table. Look at the *E. Coli* values as you go down the distance column, for example. They go up from .4 to 27.6, and then they start to go down.

These skills form the basics of graph and table reading. More complex questions will build from these fundamental skills, and this guide will cover them in the coming chapters.

RESEARCH SUMMARIES

There are three Research Summaries passages on the ACT Science Test, each with six questions.

Research Summaries passages contain a short opening description followed by short descriptions of two, three, or four experiments. Like Data Representation passages, Research Summaries passages contain graphs and tables. However, they also test your understanding of the scientific method.

As far as the ACT is concerned, the scientific method has three parts: the **purpose**, the **method**, and the **results**.

The **purpose** of an experiment is the *why*—the general principle or *hypothesis* (question) being studied. This may be how bacterial growth is affected by the presence of different nutrients, or how friction affects the amount of time it takes a rolling ball to come to a stop. Generally, the opening paragraph of a Research Summaries passage will contain the purpose. You should underline this as you first read the passage.

The **method** of an experiment is the *how*—how the researchers are finding the answer to their question. Usually, this involves changing one variable while the others are held constant. This allows researchers to isolate and study the effect of one variable at a time.

The **results** of the experiment are the *what*—the data that answer the researchers' question. These are usually printed in tables or graphs. You'll use the same skills to interpret the tables and graphs of a Research Summaries passage that you use in understanding Data Representation passages. And just like with a Data Representation passage, wait until a question requires you to study a figure. Spend your time earning points!

The questions following Research Summaries passages test both your ability to read and interpret figures (they'll be very similar to the figures questions following a Data Representation passage) and your understanding of the scientific method.

These scientific method questions might ask you, for example, to identify which factor in an experiment was varied, how changing the method might affect results, or to explain why researchers included a particular step in their method. They might also ask you to identify the hypothesis behind the experiment, whether the results support a particular hypothesis, or how new information might affect the researchers' hypothesis.

Many of the questions following a Research Summaries passage tell you exactly where to find the answer (they'll begin, "According to Experiment 1…"). Take advantage of this and answer these questions first!

In fact, the easiest way to approach a Research Summaries passage is to read the opening paragraph (or paragraphs) and Experiment 1 first. Then scan through the questions to find those that refer to *only* Experiment 1, and answer those. Next, do the same for Experiment 2 (and Experiments 3 and 4 if there are that many). Finally, answer the questions that don't reference a specific experiment. Try it! Research Summaries passages are a lot less confusing when you approach them like this.

CONFLICTING VIEWPOINTS

The last kind of passage on the ACT Science Test is called Conflicting Viewpoints. Each test contains just one of these, and it's always followed by seven questions.

Each Conflicting Viewpoints passage is structured in generally the same way. There is an opening paragraph (or two) that explains some background information about a particular phenomenon. Generally, the opening paragraph is a statement of fact. It often supplies you with a few definitions of key terms.

Next, a scientist will offer one opinion on or possible explanation for the phenomenon. A second scientist will then offer a different opinion on or explanation for the phenomenon. Sometimes, a third or fourth scientist weighs in.

Each scientist will offer different evidence to support his viewpoint. Frequently, these viewpoints will contradict each other. That's OK. Your job isn't to decide who is right and who is wrong; it's to recognize each viewpoint and understand how each scientist uses evidence to support his viewpoint.

Conflicting Viewpoints passages are different from Research Summaries or Data Representation passages; so different, in fact, that they have their own Kaplan Method.

The Kaplan Method for Conflicting Viewpoints Passages

1. **Read the introductory text and the first author's viewpoint**, then answer the questions that ask only about the first author's viewpoint.

2. **Read the second author's viewpoint**, then answer questions that ask only about the second author's viewpoint.

3. **Answer the questions that refer to both authors' viewpoints.***

   (*When there are three or more author viewpoints, you'll read each viewpoint and answer the related questions before you answer the questions that relate to multiple viewpoints.)

If you've studied the Kaplan Method for Reading passages, you may notice some similarities between the two methods. That's because Conflicting Viewpoints passages have as much in common with Reading passages as they do with Data Representation or Research Summaries passages. Use this to your advantage, too. If you prefer reading to science, start the Science Test with the Conflicting Viewpoints passage. It'll make for an easier transition. If reading's not your thing, save this one for last.

As you read the Conflicting Viewpoints passage, try to identify each scientist's hypothesis and underline it when you find it. Typically, it's right there in the first sentence. The rest of the paragraph will be devoted to evidence and supporting details.

The questions following a Conflicting Viewpoints passage test your ability to follow a scientist's line of reasoning. They might ask you why a scientist included a particular detail in his argument, or to apply a scientist's line of reasoning to a different situation. They might ask you to predict, based on what's written, what a scientist might think about a related topic.

Questions might also introduce new information and ask whether the new information weakens or strengthens one or both of the arguments. They might ask you to identify points of agreement between the two scientists (hint: look for answer choices drawn from the opening text). Conversely, a question might ask you to identify a point of disagreement.

Finally, some questions will test your reading comprehension. (They'll look something like, "According to the passage, polypeptide molecules are..." or, "The passage indicates that...") These questions are the most similar to those on the Reading Test, and you'll handle them just as you would a reading question: by going back to the passage to find your answer.

The most important thing to remember as you're taking the ACT Science Test is that answering questions, not reading the passage, earns you points. Don't get caught up in the details of a complex passage on your first read. Spend your time on the questions. That's where the payoff is.

GUESSING

Do it! There's no wrong answer penalty on the ACT. If you don't know the answer, go ahead and wager your best guess. If you can eliminate any wrong answers, you'll be in even better shape.

Chapter Twelve: **Data Representation I**

While the ACT doesn't quiz you on science terms or definitions, it does assume that you have completed at least two years of a standard three- or four-year science course of study on the college prep level. You should understand basic scientific terms and methods and be able to select data from simple and complex presentations, find information in text, and determine how one variable changes in response to another.

Let's briefly review these concepts before we get to a practice passage.

BASIC SCIENCE TERMINOLOGY

The ACT most often uses the International System of Units (SI), which includes meters (m), kilograms (kg), seconds (s), ampere (A), Kelvin (K), and mole (mol), as well as liters (L). However, it's not impossible that you'll see feet (ft), pounds (lb), or degrees Celsius (°C) or even Fahrenheit (°F). You should be comfortable using derivatives of these units as well—milliliters (mL) and grams (g), for example.

You should know what it means to create a *solution* (a mixture in which a *solute* is dissolved into a *solvent*) and to *dilute* (thin or weaken). You should understand terms such as *density* (mass per unit volume) and *force* (that which causes a mass to accelerate).

This is by no means an exhaustive list of terms you may encounter, but it represents the general level of terminology you should be comfortable with. More specific terms and pieces of equipment (such as a *bomb calorimeter*) will generally be explained within the text.

FINDING BASIC INFORMATION IN THE PASSAGE

If there's one skill that will earn you more points on the ACT Science Test than any other, it's reading data from the figures and tables. Your pencil is the key. If a question asks you to find a point on a graph, for example, draw a line up from the *x*-axis and over to the *y*-axis. You can even use a second pencil to keep your lines straight. Often, the graphs are printed pretty small, and eyeballing just isn't accurate enough.

Circle a piece of data in a table as a visual aid. The wrong answer choices usually include the values just above or below the correct one, and it's very easy for your eyes to accidentally skip up or down a row in a table.

When you're asked to find two or more pieces of data from within a figure (for example, when a question requires you to order values from least to greatest), use your pencil again. Write your answer down in your test booklet, then match it to the correct answer choice.

DETERMINING THE RELATIONSHIP BETWEEN TWO VARIABLES

If locating data within a passage is the number one skill on the ACT Science Test, then determining the relationship between two variables is number two.

Determining the relationship between two variables means observing how one variable changes in response to another. A scientist studying the relationship between the number of cars on the highway and the number of accidents, for example, will record the number of cars she counts in one hour along with the number of accidents. Then, she'll list her results in a table, with the number of cars in one column and the number of accidents in another. Or perhaps she'll graph them, with the number of cars on the *x*-axis and the number of accidents on the *y*-axis. Suppose these are her results:

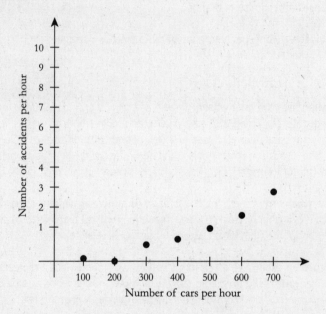

Your job is to understand by looking at the table how the number of accidents changes with the number of cars. In this example, you can see that as the number of cars increases, the number of accidents increases. That's all there is to it!

PRACTICE QUESTIONS

PASSAGE I

As the prevalence of wild wetland decreases with human population growth and urban sprawl, efforts have begun to create new wildlife habitats. In particular, scientists have studied the feasibility of conserving amphibian species by creating artificial ponds. Several studies have documented the natural process of *colonization* of artificial ponds with microorganisms (spirogyra and protozoans), aquatic plant life (*Nymphaea odorata* and *Eleocharis acisularis*), and both amphibian larvae and grown amphibians (*Hyla regilla*, *Rama sylvatica*, and *Ambystoma macrodactylum*) over time (see figure 1).

(Note: Species are organized according to their appearance over time.)

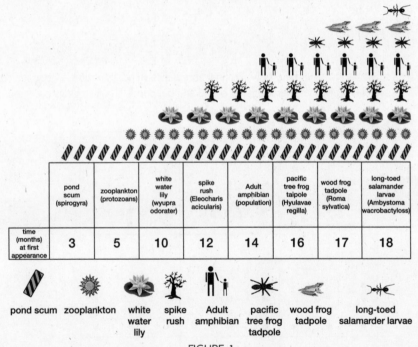

time (months) at first appearance	pond scum (spirogyra)	zooplankton (protozoans)	white water lily (wyupra odorater)	spike rush (Eleocharis acicularis)	Adult amphibian (population)	pacific tree frog taipole (Hyulavae regilla)	wood frog tadpole (Roma sylvatica)	long-toed salamander larvae (Ambystoma wacrobactyloss)
	3	5	10	12	14	16	17	18

pond scum   zooplankton   white water lily   spike rush   Adult amphibian   pacific tree frog tadpole   wood frog tadpole   long-toed salamarder larvae

FIGURE 1

As colonization progresses, amphibian larvae gradually displace vegetative cover. The larvae populations were estimated by trapping and counting the number of larvae in 1 m³ of pond water at the edge of the pond and multiplying this number by the circumference of the pond in meters. Percent vegetative cover was estimated using aerial photography to determine the fraction of pond surface area obscured by aquatic plant life. Figure 2 shows the change over time of percent vegetative cover with the advent of tadpoles and larvae in one pond.

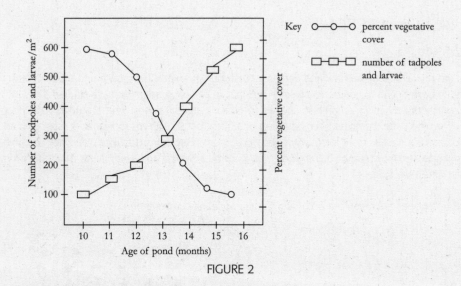

FIGURE 2

Scientists also wished to determine how the final abundance of adult amphibian species correlated with several key physical characteristics of the artificial ponds. Their findings are summarized in figure 3 below.

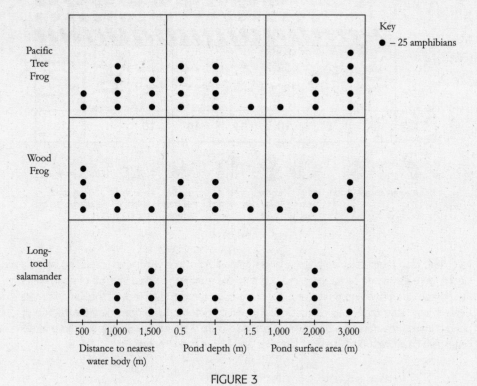

FIGURE 3

1. According to figure 1, how would the colonization of an artificial pond best be characterized at 14 months?

    A. The pond would contain a mixture of algae, aquatic plants, and amphibian larvae.

    B. The pond would contain a mixture of aquatic plants and adult amphibians.

    C. The pond would contain a mixture of algae, aquatic plants, and adult amphibians.

    D. The pond would contain a mixture of algae, amphibian larvae, and adult amphibians.

2. Given the information in figure 3, long-toed salamanders can be found in the greatest numbers in artificial ponds that:

    F. are less than 1,000 m from the nearest water body, are at least 1 m deep, and have a surface area of 2,000 m² or greater.

    G. are 1,500 m from the nearest water body, are at least 1 m deep, and have a surface area of 1000 m².

    H. are 500 m from the nearest water body, are 1.5 m deep, and have a surface area greater than 2000 m².

    J. are 1,500 m from the nearest water body, are 0.5 m deep, and have a surface area of 2000 m².

3. The passage defines *colonization* of an artificial pond as:

    A. the natural process by which algae, plant life, adult amphibians, and amphibian larvae appear in an artificial pond.

    B. the introduction by man of algae, plant life, and adult amphibians to an artificial pond.

    C. the natural arrival of predators to an artificial pond.

    D. the introduction by man of predators to an artificial pond.

4. The scientists estimated the number of amphibian larvae present in each artificial pond by:

    F. trapping and counting the number of larvae in one cubic meter of edge pond water, then multiplying by the surface area of the pond in meters squared.

    G. trapping and counting the number of larvae in one cubic meter of edge pond water, then multiplying by the circumference of the pond in meters.

    H. trapping and counting the number of larvae in one cubic meter of central pond water, then multiplying by the circumference of the pond in meters.

    J. trapping and counting the number of larvae in one cubic meter of central pond water, then multiplying by the surface area of the pond in meters squared.

5. According to information that depicts the change in percent vegetative cover and the change in amphibian larvae population, as time passes after the 10th month:

    A. the number of larvae increases and the percent vegetative cover decreases.

    B. the number of larvae increases and the percent vegetative cover increases.

    C. the number of larvae decreases and the percent vegetative cover decreases.

    D. the number of larvae decreases and the percent vegetative cover increases.

6. On the basis of the data presented in figure 1, which of the following conclusions concerning colonization is correct?

   F. Colonization of an artificial pond usually begins in winter.

   G. The final state of colonization is characterized by the presence of only plant life in the pond.

   H. Colonization of an artificial pond is characterized by an increasing diversity of plant and animal species.

   J. As colonization progresses, there is a decrease in the diversity of plant and animal species present in the pond.

7. According to the information in figure 3, the number of pacific tree frogs:

   A. stays constant as pond surface area increases.

   B. decreases as pond surface area increases.

   C. increases as pond surface area decreases.

   D. increases as pond surface area increases.

ANSWERS AND EXPLANATIONS

✓ 1. C

Here's one example of a question asking us to find one or more pieces of data in a simple data presentation. Fortunately, the question stem makes our job easy and tells us right where we need to go to find our answer; figure 1. When we look back at figure 1, we can see that algae (pond scum and zooplankton) appear between 3 and 5 months, aquatic plants (white water lily and spike rush) show up after 10 to 12 months, and an adult amphibian population is present at 14 months. That fits choice C.

We can see that choices (A) and (D) are incorrect because they state that amphibian larvae are present in the pond at 14 months. Figure 1 shows that the first amphibian larvae (pacific tree frog tadpoles) don't appear until 16 months. Choice (B) doesn't include algae, so it is likewise incorrect.

✓ 2. J

This question asks us to put together two or more pieces of data from a simple data presentation. We're directed to figure 3 and asked to figure out which artificial ponds have the most long-toed salamanders. The key beside figure 3 explains that each represents 25 amphibians.

Long-toed salamanders are represented by the bottom row in figure 3. There are 25 in ponds that are 500 m from the nearest water body, 75 in ponds 1,000 m from the nearest water body, and 100 in ponds that are 1,500 m from the nearest water body. Similarly, the maximum number of long-toed salamanders are found in ponds that are 0.5 m deep and have a surface area of 2,000 m². This fits choice (J).

✓ 3. A

This question is testing our ability to find the definition of a term used in the written part of the passage. The term *colonization* first appears in the first paragraph. It says, "Several studies have documented the natural process of *colonization* of artificial ponds with microorganisms (spirogyra and protozoans), aquatic plant life (*Nymphaea odorata* and *Eleocharis acisularis*), and both amphibian larvae and grown amphibians (*Hyla regilla*, *Rama sylvatica*, and *Ambystoma macrodactylum*) over time..." We can infer

from this sentence that the process of colonization refers to the natural process by which plants and animals come to inhabit a pond. This best matches choice (A).

We could also approach this question by examining the answer choices. Choice (B) is incorrect because it states that colonization is the "introduction by man" of plants and animals into the pond, which contradicts the information in paragraph 1. Choice (C) mentions predators, which aren't mentioned anywhere in the passage, and choice (D) mentions both introduction by man and predators, neither of which is supported by the passage. That leaves us with just choice (A).

✗ 4. G

This question is testing our ability to understand the scientists' methods. Numbers of amphibian larvae are shown on the left-hand axis of figure 2, so we should start by reading the paragraph just before figure 2. It states that, "The larvae populations were estimated by trapping and counting the larvae in 1 m³ of pond water at the edge of the pond and multiplying this number by the circumference of the pond in meters." This is correctly restated in choice (G).

Notice that only subtle changes make the other choices incorrect. Choice (F) substitutes surface area for circumference, choice (H) substitutes central pond water for edge water, and choice (J) makes both substitutions.

✓ 5. A

This kind of question asks us to determine how variables change over time. Figure 2 shows how the percentage of vegetative cover changes with the population of larvae, so that's where we should look for our answer. Notice that the question stem restricts us to "after 12 months." This makes our job easier, because from 10 to 12 months, the percentage of vegetative cover is steady. After 12 months, we can see that as the population of larvae increase, the percentage of vegetative cover steadily drops. This matches choice (A).

6. H

Here is an example of a question that asks us to draw "conclusions" from a figure. In this case, that's really just another way to ask us to state what the figure shows. So what does figure 1 show? That as time goes by, an artificial pond becomes home to first algae and plankton, then plant life, and finally animals. The icons accompanying figure 1 indicate that none of these species entirely replaces another. Rather, the pond becomes home to an increasingly diverse population of plants and animals. This matches choice (H).

There is no information in the entire passage that supports choice (F). Choice (G) is incorrect because the final state of colonization is characterized by the presence of both plant and animal life, and choice (J) is incorrect because it states the opposite of what figure 1 shows.

7. D

We can save ourselves a little time by looking at the answer choices before we answer this question. It's clear that we need to compare the pacific tree frog population to pond surface area. That's depicted in the third column of the first row of figure 3. We can see that the number of frogs increases as the surface area of the pond increases. Choice (D) is correct.

Chapter Thirteen: **Data Representation II**

Answering the questions that accompany Data Representation passages will also require more complex skills that build upon the ones covered in chapter 12. To do well on these passages, you must be able to locate data within complex presentations, compare or combine data points from one, two, or more simple or complex presentations, translate information into a table, graph, or diagram, interpolate between data points, and determine the relationship between two variables in a complex presentation.

LOCATING DATA WITHIN COMPLEX PRESENTATIONS

Nothing is more intimidating than a science chart with lots of lines heading in all different directions, except for maybe a chart with lots of lines and a few random Greek letters. But keep your cool! The ACT doesn't expect that you have your Ph.D. The complex charts and graphs might look scary, but remind yourself that they're designed to be comprehensible to high school students just like you.

As you read the passage containing the complex figure for the first time, read the paragraph preceding the figure for an explanation of what it shows. Read the axis labels and any legend or key accompanying the figure, but then stop there.

When a question asks you specifically about the complex figure, the key is to focus only on the relevant information and block out everything else that's going on. Often, complex figures are only complex because they show how more than one variable behaves at a time. Use your pencil to trace only the curve that applies to the question at hand and you'll find that the figure often isn't really as complex as it first appeared.

COMPARING AND COMBINING DATA

You might be asked to combine or compare data from simple presentations. To compare data, circle all of the relevant points in the graph or table. This will help you to focus on only what's asked and exclude any possible distractions. Most often, questions of this type will ask you to order from least to greatest (or vice versa). For example, you may be shown a table that lists the viscosity of several liquids, and asked to order them from most to least viscous.

Other questions will ask you to combine data. Usually, this just means adding or subtracting the numbers. These questions will often ask you to find the difference between two data points.

Remember that on a first read, some questions (like some figures) will appear pretty complicated. Remind yourself that complicated questions are really just questions that ask you to put together a few simple steps. Take the question one step at a time, and you'll find that getting the answer is much easier than it first appeared.

TRANSLATING INFORMATION INTO A TABLE, GRAPH, OR DIAGRAM

Occasionally, a question will ask you to generate your own graph, table, or diagram. This sounds difficult, but these are usually among the easier questions in a passage. That's because a) the graphs are usually very straightforward, and b) you don't actually have to generate them. You just have to pick the correct plot out of four choices.

To identify the correct plot, first check the general trend of the data by looking at the slope of the curve or the values in the table. Is the data you're looking for increasing, decreasing, or staying the same? Match the shape you're looking for to the answer choices.

If more than one choice remains after you check the trends, check individual values. If the information in the passage indicates that the data should have a specific value at a given point, look for the choice that contains that point. It shouldn't take more than a few seconds to backtrack your way to the correct answer.

INTERPOLATING POINTS

Interpolation simply means "reading between." Some questions will ask you to approximate values in between those actually shown in the passage. Again, this is a lot easier than it sounds.

Suppose, for example, a passage contains a table—say, one that lists distance in multiples of 10 cm in one column and corresponding intensity in the other—and you're asked to find the intensity at 15 cm. Your job would be to look for the values of intensity at 10 cm and 20 cm, and make a guess halfway in between those. Easy!

If you're looking at a graph, the task is similar. Look for the values just below and above the point in question, and make a guess somewhere in the middle. Then, simply match your guess to the answer choices.

UNDERSTANDING THE RELATIONSHIP BETWEEN VARIABLES IN A COMPLEX DATA PRESENTATION

Understanding the relationship between variables will remain a primary skill in passages with complex data presentations. The basic methods are the same as those discussed in chapter 12 of this guide, but you'll have to focus harder to zero in on the variables you need and ignore the ones you don't.

Work methodically. Locate one variable at a time (check the axes of a graph, or the left-most column and top row of a table, for your variables). If you can't find them, look for the appropriate units: If a question asks for temperature, look for °C or °F.

When you find your variables, ask yourself how one changes as the other increases or decreases. Then match your answer to the choices. Again, these complex questions often reduce to a series of a few simple steps. Take them one step at a time and you'll find getting the answer is far easier than it looks!

PRACTICE QUESTIONS

PASSAGE II

Table 1 below shows the percent composition of Earth's atmosphere by volume*, temperature, and pressure according to elevation above a specific location. An elevation of 0 kilometers represents sea level, the surface of Earth. Temperature is given in degrees Celsius, and pressure in mmHg.

Atmospheric layer	Elevation (km)	Pressure (mmHg)	Temperature (°C)	Concentration (% by volume)				
				N_2	O_2	He	H_2	H_2O
Troposphere	0	1000	25	78.08	20.94	0.0005	0.00005	2
	15	100	−45	78.08	20.94	0.0005	0.00005	1
Stratosphere	50	10	−5	78.08	20.94	0.0005	0.00005	0.25
Mesosphere	90	3	−90	78.08	20.94	0.0005	0.00005	0
Thermosphere	200	1	900	0	99.78	0.0005	0.00005	0
	500	0.001	1,500	0	0	99.6	0.4	0
Exosphere	1000	0.0001	0	0	0	0.05	99.05	0

*Percent composition by volume is equivalent to the mole-fraction of the gas—i.e., the number of molecules of the gas over the total number of molecules in any given volume.

The temperature in Earth's atmosphere does not vary continuously with elevation. Figure 1 below shows the complex relationship between elevation and temperature in Earth's atmosphere.

Image and associated databases are available from the National Oceanic and Atmospheric Administration, U.S. Department of Commerce, www.srh.noaa.gov/srh/jetstream/atmos/atmprofile.htm.

1. According to the data presented in table 1, what is the percent concentration of O_2 at 50 km?

    A. 99.78

    B. 78.08

    C. 20.94

    D. 0.005

2. The percent concentrations of which of the following gases are constant below an elevation of 90 km?

F. N_2, O_2, and H_2O only

G. H_2O only

H. N_2, O_2, and H_2 only

J. N_2, O_2, He, and H_2 only

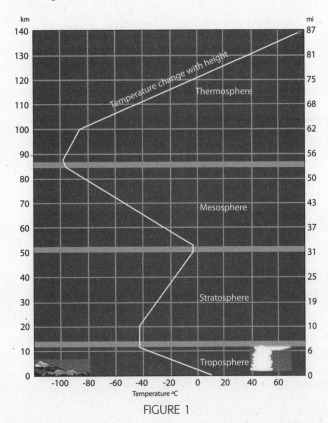

FIGURE 1

Image and associated databases are available from the National Oceanic and Atmospheric Administration, U.S. Department of Commerce, www.srh.noaa.gov/srh/jetstream/atmos/atmprofile.htm.

3. Which of the following graphs represents the relationship between O_2 concentration and elevation?

A.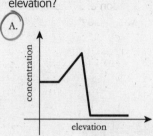

B.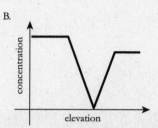

C.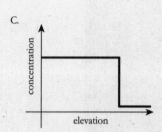

D.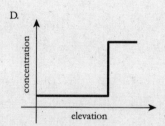

4. According to table 1, the concentration of H_2O at 10 km is approximately:

   F. 1%

   G. 1.5%

   H. 2%

   J. 10%

5. A group of researchers sent up a weather balloon from their lab. The balloon sent back a temperature reading of −20°C. Given the information in figure 1, which of the following elevations could possibly be the elevation of the balloon?

   A. 7 km

   B. 23 km, 59 km, or 116 km

   C. 23 km, 37 km, 59 km, or 116 km

   D. 7 km, 37 km, 59 km, or 116 km

6. Suppose a rocket malfunctions on its way into outer space. The last readings the rocket sent to Earth before the malfunction were an atmospheric O_2 concentration of 33.75%, an H_2O concentration of 0%, and a temperature of −85°C. At what elevation did the rocket likely malfunction?

   F. 10 km

   G. 50 km

   H. 100 km

   J. 500 km

7. According to the information in figure 1, between 50 and 85 km, as elevation increases:

   A. temperature increases.

   B. temperature decreases.

   C. temperature decreases, then increases.

   D. temperature increases, then decreases.

ANSWERS AND EXPLANATIONS

1. C

This is a classic example of a question asking us to locate data from within a complex data presentation. Table 1 has nine rows and nine columns, and contains an awful lot of information. To zero in on the data we need to answer this question, we should start by looking for the column labeled "O_2." (Hint: it's the sixth column.) Then, use a pencil to follow that column down until we reach the 50 km row. Underline the 50 km row, and see where it meets the line down the O_2 row. It's easy for your eyes to accidentally skip up, down, or over a row in such a big table, so marking the row and column you need will help avoid unnecessary errors. The correct answer is choice (C), 20.94%.

2. J

Here's a great example of a comparing data question. The question asks us to list the gases with constant concentrations below an elevation of 90 km. To answer, we need to underline the 90 km row in table 1 (again, this makes it easier to keep track of). Which gases have concentrations that don't change above this line? N_2, O_2, He, and H_2. The correct answer is choice (J).

Choice (G) is a trap. Notice that the question stem asks for concentrations "below an elevation of 90 km". Below 90 km means less than 90 km, which on the table means the rows *above* 90 km. If we had read that "below" literally, and read down on the table, we might have picked choice (J).

3. A

This question asks us to translate information from a table into a graph. Looking at the answer choices, we can see that the graph we are asked to generate doesn't contain specific points (in fact, there are no numbers at all on any of the graphs in the answer choices), merely an approximation of the general shape of the curve we would expect to see.

To find the correct graph, look at the column for O_2 concentration in figure 1 (that's the sixth column from the left). From 0 to 90 km, concentration remains constant at 20.94%. Then, at 200 km, it spikes to 99.6%. Above 500 km, it's 0%.

Choice (A) best represents this trend. Notice that choice (D) shows the steep rise, but not the drop back down to zero, and choice (C) shows the drop down to zero, but not the steep rise to 99.6%.

4. G

This question tests our ability to interpolate two data points. Table 1 doesn't directly give us a value for percent H_2O concentration at 10 km, but it does give us the percent concentrations at 0 and 15 km (which are 2% and 1%, respectively). Our job is to read in between the lines. Since 10 km is between 0 and 15 km, we need to find the answer choice between 2% and 1%. That's choice (G).

5. D

Here's another question testing our ability to combine data from a complex presentation. The curve in figure 1 zigzags a few times, and crosses over −20°C more than once. To identify the elevations that could measure −20°C, we should draw a line up from −20°C on the x-axis. We can see that the line intersects the curve four times. Tracing left to the y-axis from those four points of intersection, we can see that possible elevations at −20°C are approximately 7 km, 37 km, 59 km, and 116 km. That matches choice (D).

6. H

This question requires us to combine information from two complex sources: table 1 and figure 1. Our first clue is that the O_2 concentration at the elevation of malfunction is 33.75%. The O_2 concentration is given in table 1, so we should start by checking there; it shows that the O_2 concentration rises from 20.94% above 90 km. Without going any further, we know we can eliminate choices (F) and (G). Our rocket is definitely above these elevations.

Our next clues are an H_2O concentration of 0% and a temperature of −85°C. The H_2O concentration is 0% for any elevation above 90 km, so that doesn't give us any additional information. Temperature, however, is an important clue. According to figure 1, a temperature of −85°C only occurs above 90 km once, at about 100 km. Choice (H), then, is the correct answer.

7. B

Here's a question asking us to understand the relation-ship between variables in a complex data presentation. Fortunately, this question makes our job a bit easier by restricting elevation to between 50 and 85 km. We should start by drawing a horizontal line through 50 km, and a second horizontal line through 85 km. Now we can focus on only the relevant section of the curve.

We can see clearly that between our two lines, as elevation increases, temperature decreases. This is stated in choice (B).

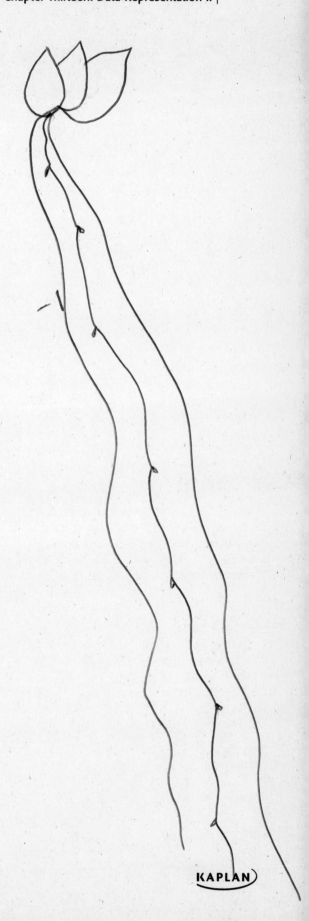

Chapter Fourteen: **Data Representation III**

The final set of skills required for Data Representation passages includes selecting hypotheses, conclusions, or predictions supported by the data, comparing and combining data from complex sources, identifying and using complex relationships between variables, and extrapolating from the data. Don't let the sound of these terms scare you—as usual, they break down into a few relatively simple steps. Zeroing in on exactly which variables are addressed in the question stem and finding the relevant part of the passage will take you 90% of the way to the correct answer.

SELECTING HYPOTHESES, CONCLUSIONS, OR PREDICTIONS FROM THE DATA

Remember from chapter 11 that a hypothesis is the question a researcher is testing and a conclusion is the answer to that question that is suggested by the data. Occasionally, you'll be asked to identify valid hypotheses or conclusions based on what is written in the passage. Remember, the answer is always right there under your nose! Your job is never more complicated than distinguishing the correct choice from among three choices that *must* be wrong.

To answer these questions, first go back to the passage. Find where it discusses the information in the question stem, and see if you can predict the answer. If you can, great. If you can't, then see if you can identify the fatal flaw in each of the incorrect answer choices. Often, these flaws will be pretty obvious: Some choices might reference information that has absolutely nothing to do with the passage; some might reference an unrelated detail from another part of the passage; still others might reverse the correct relationship.

COMPARING AND COMBINING DATA FROM COMPLEX PRESENTATIONS

Comparing and combining data from complex presentations isn't any more difficult than comparing and combining data from simple presentations. What's harder is *finding* the appropriate data in the midst of a complex presentation.

What makes a presentation complex? Usually, it's the presence of lots of variables in one giant table, a bizarre-looking graph with three or more lines, at least one of which is zigzagging, and some kind of strange units, especially angstroms (Å) (that's 0.1 nanometer, usually used for wavelength).

To find the right data in a complex presentation, use the skills discussed in chapter 13: look to the axes to find units (which can point you to the correct variable) and use your pencil to highlight only the appropriate data. Then, focus on the precise calculation the question stem is asking for. Sometimes you'll need to figure out which piece of data is bigger, or rank the data from least to greatest. Sometimes you'll have to add or subtract values. The actual calculations you make will be very simple. Calculators aren't allowed on the Science Test, and you'll never need them.

IDENTIFYING AND USING COMPLEX RELATIONSHIPS BETWEEN VARIABLES

ACT Science focuses on the relationship between variables. Often, those relationships are pretty straightforward; as one variable increases by a constant amount, the other increases or decreases by a constant amount. Occasionally, the relationship will be more complex; as one variable doubles, for example, the other will quadruple. This is known as an *exponential* relationship, and is the most common sort of complex relationship on the ACT.

If you suspect a complex relationship between variables, be sure to look at more than one data point. For example, if doubling the quantity of a solution quadruples the reaction time, check to see what tripling the quantity does (it should multiply the reaction time by nine). Take those extra few seconds to make sure you're seeing what you think you're seeing.

Using the complex relationships is simpler than identifying them. Once you've nailed down the relationship between the two variables, use that to predict what will happen next.

EXTRAPOLATING FROM DATA

Extrapolating from data means predicting the value of a data point that falls beyond the range given. The rule here is to assume the data trends continue as indicated by the table or graph. If you see a line graphed as straight from 1 to 100 on the *x*-axis, assume it continues to be straight. If it's a curve that's beginning to level off at the top, assume that leveling trend continues. If a table shows a variable steadily increasing, you can safely assume that subsequent values not shown on the table continue to increase.

PRACTICE QUESTIONS

PASSAGE III

Sunburn is a serious reaction to excess sun exposure. Figure 1 shows effects of sunburn on the body from the time of exposure until six days post-exposure. Following excess sun exposure, the body begins to produce melanin, a pigment that helps protect skin cells from further sun damage. Figure 1 shows levels of melanin production in the skin following sun exposure.

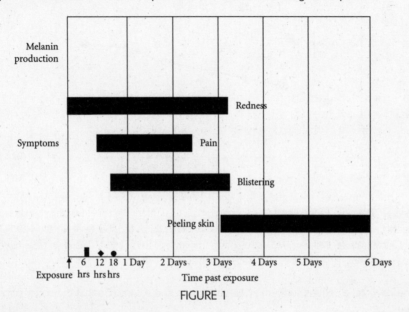

FIGURE 1

Sun exposure is also suspected to contribute to melanoma, a particularly deadly form of skin cancer. The frequency of melanoma reported in the United States among populations that have suffered at least one blistering sunburn and among populations that have never suffered a blistering sunburn are shown below in figure 2.

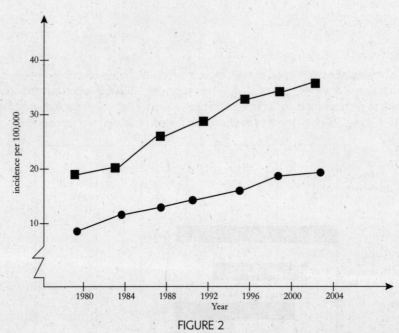

FIGURE 2

Figure adapted from Ries LAG, Melbert D, Krapcho M, Mariotto A, Miller BA, Feuer EJ, Clegg L, Horner MJ, Howlader N, Eisner MP, Reichman M, Edwards BK (eds). SEER Cancer Statistics Review, 1975–2004, National Cancer Institute. Bethesda, MD, www.seer.cancer.gov/csr/1975_2004/, based on November 2006 SEER data submission, posted to the SEER website, 2007.

1. One day after a serious sunburn is sustained, one could conclude that the major symptoms would be:
   A. redness, pain, and peeling skin.
   B. redness, pain, and blistering.
   C. pain, blistering, and peeling skin.
   D. redness, pain, blistering, and peeling skin.

2. Suffering just one blistering sunburn has which of the following, if any, effects on the chance of developing melanoma?
   F. It doubles an individual's chance of developing melanoma.
   G. It triples an individual's chance of developing melanoma.
   H. It decreases an individual's chance of developing melanoma by one half.
   J. It has no effect on an individual's chance of developing melanoma.

3. Several students spent a day at the beach and suffered serious sunburns. According to the information in the passage and in figure 1, should these students expect to be fully recovered within four days?
   A. Yes, all symptoms will have resolved within four days.
   B. Yes, only blistering is expected to remain at four days.
   C. No, the students will still be suffering from blisters and peeling skin within four days.
   D. No, the students will still be suffering from peeling skin only within four days.

4. Based on the data in figure 1, one can conclude that the body's production of melanin peaks:

    F. 6 hours after sun exposure.

    G. 12 hours after sun exposure.

    H. 24 hours after sun exposure.

    J. 2 days after sun exposure.

5. Assume that sustaining a blistering burn causes people to develop melanoma within one year. If approximately 1 in 100 people who develop a blistering burn go on to develop melanoma, approximately what was the incidence of blistering burns per 100,000 people in 1980?

    A. 2,000

    B. 1,000

    C. 200

    D. 100

6. Which years showed the sharpest increase in incidence of melanoma among populations who have experienced a blistering sunburn?

    F. 2000–2004

    G. 1996–2000

    H. 1988–1992

    J. 1984–1988

7. According to the information in figure 2, approximately what incidence of melanoma can be expected in 2008 among people who have never experienced a blistering sunburn?

    A. 35/100,000

    B. 19/100,000

    C. 35/10,000

    D. 19/10,000

ANSWERS AND EXPLANATIONS

1. B

To find the conclusion that is supported by the passage, we must go back to where sunburn symptoms are discussed in the passage. A quick glance tells us that's figure 1.

According to the figure, redness, pain, and blistering will be present after one day. This matches choice (B). Note that peeling skin doesn't occur until after three days, making choices (A), (C), and (D) incorrect.

2. F

Here is another comparing and combining data question. To determine the effect that experiencing a blistering sunburn has on a person's chances of developing melanoma, we need to check figure 2. Specifically, we must compare the odds of a person getting melanoma after experiencing a blistering sunburn to the odds of a person getting melanoma after never experiencing a blistering sunburn. To do that, we should compare a few points on the graph.

Let's look, for example, at the odds of a person getting melanoma in 1980. Nonblistering sunburn people have about a 9.5/100,000 chance of getting it, versus a 19/100,000 chance for those with a blistering sunburn. That means one blistering sunburn about doubles your chances for getting melanoma. If we check a few other points, we can see that this relationship is consistent through 2004. That matches choice (F).

Note that we can't answer this question by simply eyeballing the answer. That's because the y-axis of figure 2 doesn't start at 0, but at 9. Researchers often "edit out" a section of one axis (most often the y-axis) to save space. That's what makes this figure complex, and that's why it's so important that we actually compare the values at a few different points.

3. D

Here's a question that asks us to make a prediction based on the information in the passage. Because symptoms are shown in figure 1, we should start there.

Figure 1 tells us that four days after a serious sunburn, only peeling skin should remain as a symptom. This matches choice (D).

4. H

Melanin production is shown on the top of figure 1. The curve rises steeply until one day after the initial exposure, then begins to taper off gradually. This tells us that the body's production of melanin peaks 24 hours after exposure, choice (H).

5. A

Mathematically speaking, this is as complex as questions get on the ACT Science Test. By working through it slowly and methodically, we can see that finding the answer is not exceptionally difficult.

First, we should make sure we understand exactly what the question is asking us to do—find the incidence of *blistering burns* per 100,000 people in 1980. Figure 2 gives us the incidence of *melanoma* per 100,000 people who have previously suffered a blistering burn in 1980 (about 20/100,000). How can we get from the incidence of *melanoma* to the incidence of *blistering burns* themselves? The question stem provides the link. It says that about 1 in 100 people who develop a blistering burn go on to develop melanoma that year. If 20 in 100,000 people developed melanoma, the incidence of blistering burns must have been 100 times higher, or 2,000 per 100,000. Choice (A) is correct.

6. H

To answer this question, we should use the answer choices to limit the amount of work we need to do. The sharpest increase must occur between 2000 to 2004, 1996 to 2000, 1988 to 1992, or 1984 to 1988. Figure 2 shows a fairly slow increase in melanoma rates for the blistering sunburn population (represented with squares) from 1996 to 2004, so eliminate choices (F) and (G). The line segment from 1984 to 1988 has a slope that is obviously steeper than the segment that connects 1988 to 1992, so choice (H) is correct.

7.　B

Here's a great example of a question that requires us to extrapolate from a graph. Values for 2008 aren't plotted on figure 2, so we have to use the information in the figure to wager our best guess.

The most important thing to do is make sure we're looking at the right line on the graph. The question is asking us for prevalence among those who have "never experienced a blistering sunburn," a population represented by the line with circles. The figure shows a value of about 18/100,000 in 2000 and a little more than that—maybe 18.5/100,000—in 2004. We can guess, then, that choice (B), 19/100,000, will be the rate in 2008.

Chapter Fifteen: **Research Summaries I**

Research Summaries passages build on the skills tested by Data Representation passages. While they continue to contain questions that test your ability to find and interpret data, they'll also test your understanding of and ability to use the scientific method: the purpose, methods, and results of an experiment. We'll examine these question types closely in the next three chapters.

UNDERSTANDING THE TOOLS IN A SIMPLE EXPERIMENT

As explained in chapter 11, Research Summaries passages will typically consist of an opening paragraph explaining some background information and the basic setup of the experiment, followed by two or more short descriptions of the specifics of the experiments researchers conducted and their results. The opening paragraph or experiment descriptions might contain a complex-looking diagram, like this one:

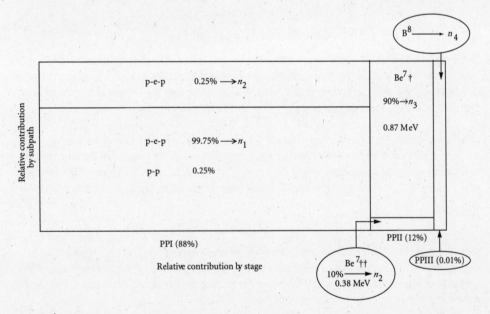

The experiment descriptions will always be followed by the results that particular experiment achieved.

Some of the experimental setup diagrams will look pretty unfamiliar and complicated. Don't let that panic you! Treat them like you would any other figure on the ACT: summarize the gist of it, and then move on. You can look at it in more detail when you come to a question that relates to it. If you saw the figure above, for example, it'd be enough to note that you were looking at the diagram of a simple circuit. That's all!

Other tools involved in a simple experiment are the same tools you've used in your high school science labs. Remember, the ACT assumes you've taken at least two years of college-prep-level science, and that usually includes a certain amount of lab work. You should be familiar with what it means to measure temperature, measure quantities of liquids, record masses, record physical observations, and carry out many of the other routine tasks required by a high school science lab.

UNDERSTANDING A SIMPLE EXPERIMENTAL DESIGN

Some of the questions following a Research Summaries passage will test your ability to understand how an experiment was put together. Typically, this will require you to understand the researchers' methods. Ask yourself, "How did they set up their experiment? Which were the variables that the researchers changed? Which variables changed in response? What did the researchers record in their results?"

Remember that experiments on the ACT, while they may look complicated at first glance, are usually very straightforward. Some basic equipment will be set up and a few trials will be run. Only a handful of variables will be manipulated. Remind yourself that the passages usually look much harder at first glance than they really are.

IDENTIFYING A CONTROL IN AN EXPERIMENT

There are two terms that you may not see often on the ACT, but it's helpful to know them anyway: independent and dependent variables. **Independent variables** are the variables deliberately manipulated by researchers. **Dependent variables** are those that are observed to change in response to the independent variables.

When researchers are trying to figure out the effects of the independent variables they're studying, they'll want to weed out effects caused by other variables they're not thinking of or measuring—the humidity of the room if it's a chemistry experiment, the amount of rainfall this year if it's an outdoor biology experiment, or any other factor that's not in their control or on their radar.

To do this, they'll usually run what's called a *control*. Think of this as a "blank" experiment of sorts; the experiment run without any of the independent variables in it at all. For example, if researchers are measuring how three patches of sunflowers grow when they're fed three different kinds of nutrient solutions, they'll often plant a fourth patch of sunflowers fed only water. The water-fed patch would be the experiment's control.

IDENTIFYING SIMILARITIES AND DIFFERENCES BETWEEN EXPERIMENTS

Questions asking you to identify the similarities and differences between experiments are a guarantee on the ACT, but luckily, finding the answer is really straightforward. Usually, it's printed in the paragraph below the *Experiment 1, 2,* or *3* headings. Often, you'll see an explanation of Experiment 2 along the lines of "Scientists repeated Experiment 1, but brought the temperature of the solution to 25°C." Then, looking at the description of Experiment 1, you'll find that the scientists ran that experiment at 15°C.

You should also look quickly at the results the scientists achieved with each experiment. These are almost always printed in tables in Research Summaries passages, and the tables are usually pretty small (the big, monster tables are found in Data Representation passages). Column 1 usually contains the independent variables and column 2 the dependent variables. If the column 1s of the two tables match, you'll know that the researchers ran basically the same experiment again, with one minor difference. If the column 1s are different, you'll know that the researchers varied more than just the temperature at which the experiment was run.

PRACTICE QUESTION

PASSAGE I

Friction is the force acting between two surfaces in contact with each other. Students wished to determine the amount of force required to overcome the force of friction between two unmoving objects. To conduct their experiment, they rested a block of wood on top of a larger wooden plane. Next, they set a weight atop the wooden block. Then, a tangential force was applied to the wooden block and measured with a spring scale, as diagrammed in figure 1. The tangential force required to cause the wooden block to begin sliding across the plane was recorded.

(Note: Assume the mass of the spring scale is insignificant.)

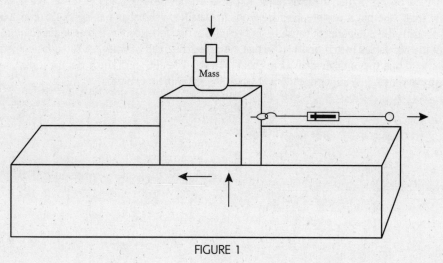

FIGURE 1

Experiment 1

Students placed a wooden block with a surface area of 100 cm^2 in the apparatus depicted above. A tangential force was applied, and the force at which the block began to slip was recorded in newtons (N). The experiment was repeated using weights of differing masses atop the wooden block. The forces required to cause the wooden block to slip were recorded in table 1.

Table 1

Mass of Weight (kg)	Tangential Force (N)
0.5	6.1
1.0	12.3
1.5	18.8
2.0	24.5
2.5	30.6

Experiment 2

Experiment 1 was repeated using a wooden block of the same mass as in Experiment 1, but a surface area of 200 cm². The mass of the weight atop the block was varied as in Experiment 1, and the tangential forces required to cause the block to slip were recorded in table 2 below.

Table 2

Mass of Weight (kg)	Tangential Force (N)
0.5	6.1
1.0	12.3
1.5	18.8
2.0	24.5
2.5	30.6

Experiment 3

In this experiment, the coefficient of friction between the wooden block and the plane was lowered by the application of grease to the plane. The procedures from Experiment 1 were repeated using the wooden block and weights from Experiment 1.

Table 3

Mass of Weight (kg)	Tangential Force (N)
0.5	3.6
1.0	6.2
1.5	9.4
2.0	12.3
2.5	15.3

1. Which of the following statements best explains why the students varied the mass of the weight atop the wooden block in Experiment 1? The students wanted to:

   A. measure the amount of downward force between the wooden block and the plane.

   B. vary the amount of tangential force on the wooden block.

   C. study how different materials affect friction.

   D. vary downward force between the wooden block and the plane.

2. In Experiment 1, students varied which of the following factors?

   F. the surface area of the wooden block.

   G. the mass atop the wooden block.

   H. the length of the plane.

   J. the composition of the plane.

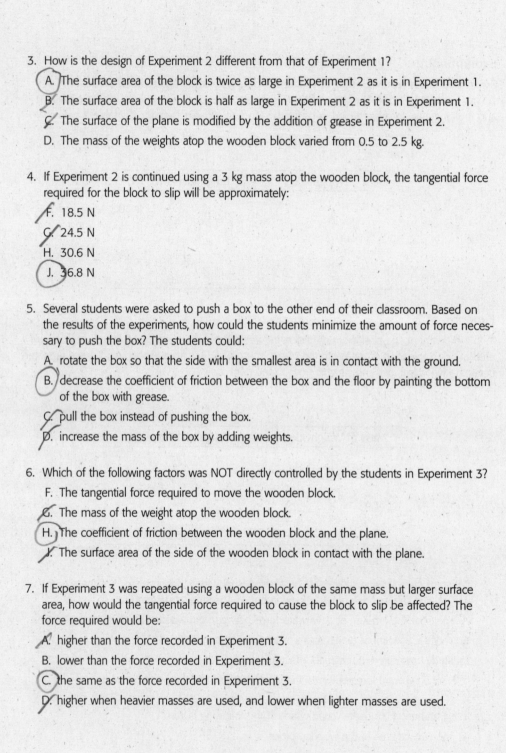

3. How is the design of Experiment 2 different from that of Experiment 1?

   A. The surface area of the block is twice as large in Experiment 2 as it is in Experiment 1.

   B. The surface area of the block is half as large in Experiment 2 as it is in Experiment 1.

   C. The surface of the plane is modified by the addition of grease in Experiment 2.

   D. The mass of the weights atop the wooden block varied from 0.5 to 2.5 kg.

4. If Experiment 2 is continued using a 3 kg mass atop the wooden block, the tangential force required for the block to slip will be approximately:

   F. 18.5 N

   G. 24.5 N

   H. 30.6 N

   J. 36.8 N

5. Several students were asked to push a box to the other end of their classroom. Based on the results of the experiments, how could the students minimize the amount of force necessary to push the box? The students could:

   A. rotate the box so that the side with the smallest area is in contact with the ground.

   B. decrease the coefficient of friction between the box and the floor by painting the bottom of the box with grease.

   C. pull the box instead of pushing the box.

   D. increase the mass of the box by adding weights.

6. Which of the following factors was NOT directly controlled by the students in Experiment 3?

   F. The tangential force required to move the wooden block.

   G. The mass of the weight atop the wooden block.

   H. The coefficient of friction between the wooden block and the plane.

   J. The surface area of the side of the wooden block in contact with the plane.

7. If Experiment 3 was repeated using a wooden block of the same mass but larger surface area, how would the tangential force required to cause the block to slip be affected? The force required would be:

   A. higher than the force recorded in Experiment 3.

   B. lower than the force recorded in Experiment 3.

   C. the same as the force recorded in Experiment 3.

   D. higher when heavier masses are used, and lower when lighter masses are used.

ANSWERS AND EXPLANATIONS

1. D

This question tests our understanding of the experimental design. What was the point of putting weights on top of the wooden block? The students wanted to be able to increase the downward force of the wooden block without changing the wooden block itself. By placing different masses on top of the same wooden block, they could increase or decrease the downward force between the wooden block and the plane. Choice (D) is correct.

2. G

Look at table 1. It shows how the tangential force required to cause the block to slip changes as the mass of the weight atop the block increases. This information is also in the paragraph before table 1 (look at the sentence that reads, "The experiment was repeated using weights of differing masses atop the wooden block.") Choice (G) is correct.

Choice (F) is incorrect because the students kept the surface area of the wooden block that was in contact with the plane constant at 100 cm². This varied between Experiment 1 and Experiment 2, so answering this question after reading only Experiment 1 helps us avoid confusion.

3. A

Here is a question that tests our ability to distinguish the differences between two experiments. To answer, we should first look at the paragraph underneath the Experiment 2 heading. It reads, "Experiment 1 was repeated using a wooden block of the same mass as in Experiment 1, but a surface area of 200 cm²." The surface area of the wooden block in contact with the plane was 100 cm² in Experiment 1, so the correct choice is (A). Note that choice (B) reverses the relationship between surface area in the experiments and is therefore incorrect.

Choice (C) is incorrect because it states the difference between Experiments 1 and 3, and choice (D) is incorrect because both experiments varied the mass of the weights atop the wooden blocks. It represents something that is the same in both experiments, not different.

4. J

Research Summaries passages will have a few of the same question types that we see in Data Representation passages. Here, we're asked to extrapolate from table 2. Answer this question after reading Experiment 2, but before looking at Experiment 3. The mass of the weight in table 2 varies from 0.5 to 2.5 kg, and the tangential force increases steadily as the mass increases. Because the tangential force required to move a block with a 2.5 kg mass atop it is 30.6 N, and each 0.5 kg increase results in an approximately 6 N increase in tangential force, we need an answer choice close to 36 N. Only choice (J) fits the bill.

5. B

To answer this question, we'll have to draw from the passage as a whole, so it's best to save this one for last, when our understanding of the passage will be most complete.

According to the passage, which factors lead to a decrease in the amount of tangential force required to move a block (or, in this case, a box)? Experiment 1 shows us that decreasing the downward force on the box will make it easier to push, but this doesn't match any of the answer choices. In fact, choice (D) states the exact opposite of this idea, so we can eliminate it.

Experiment 2 shows us that, contrary to what our intuition might tell us, increasing the surface area does not increase the amount of tangential force required to move the box. Rotating the box so that the side with the smallest area is in contact with the ground, then, won't make it any easier to push, and we can eliminate choice (A).

Experiment 3 shows us that decreasing the coefficient of friction between two surfaces by spreading one with grease decreases the tangential force needed to push a block. Spreading one side of the box with grease, however messy, would then make the box easier to push, so choice (B) is correct.

Note that the passage never mentioned the difference between a push and a pull, so choice (C) must be incorrect as well.

6. F

The key to answering this question correctly is the phrase "directly controlled" in the question stem. While all of the answer choices represent variables that changed over the course of Experiment 3, only one was NOT "directly" controlled by the students; the tangential force required to move the wooden block, choice (F).

The precise terms here are "dependent" and "independent" variables. Independent variables are deliberately manipulated by researchers. Dependent variables are those that are observed to change in response to the independent variables.

In Experiment 3, the mass of the weight atop the wooden block is an independent variable, directly manipulated by the students. The coefficient of friction between the wooden block and the plane was directly manipulated by the students through the application of grease, and the surface area of the wooden block in contact with the plane was also directly controlled by the students. Note that these variables don't need to be changed over the course of the experiment to be directly controlled by the experimenters—holding something constant is also a way of controlling it.

Only the tangential force required to move the wooden block changed in response to another variable (the mass of the weight atop the block), so only this was not directly controlled by the students. The tangential force was a dependent variable, and so choice (F) is correct.

7. C

Here is a question that requires us to apply the results of one experiment to another. To find out how surface area affects tangential force, we should look to Experiments 1 and 2. Tables 1 and 2 show that when the students doubled the area of contact between the wooden block and the plane, the tangential force remained unchanged.

We would expect, then, that increasing the area of contact in Experiment 3 would have no effect on tangential force. Choice (C) is correct.

Chapter Sixteen: **Research Summaries II**

Research Summaries passages test your ability to understand the purpose, method, and results of experiments in many different ways. In this chapter, you'll learn how to identify additional trials or experiments that can be performed to enhance or evaluate experimental results; predict the results of these additional trials or measurements; predict how modifying the design of an experiment could effect its results; determine which experimental conditions would produce specific results; and analyze the given information.

ADDITIONAL TRIALS AND EXPERIMENTS

The Research Summaries passages on your ACT might contain questions asking you to take the experiments one step further by identifying trials or experiments that would give researchers more information. To answer these questions correctly, you must understand how experiments are set up and recognize the independent and dependent variables. If you don't remember what those terms mean, go back right now and reread chapter 15!

The secret to answering questions about new trials or experiments is to determine, from the question stem, exactly what the researchers need to know that they don't already. Then, all you have to do is identify which answer choice addresses just this variable, while keeping the others constant. Watch out for answer choices that identify variables already explored in previous trials or experiments—they're there to confuse you by looking familiar. People are drawn to wrong answers that look familiar. Also avoid answer choices that stray too far from the topic. People are likewise drawn to answer choices that look confusing and complicated.

Other questions will ask you to predict the results of a hypothetical new trial or experiment. These questions are very similar to the questions that accompany Data Representation passages because they require you to recognize patterns and trends in the data. The key in these is to identify *which* patterns and trends apply to the question at hand. The question stem will give you clues to figure out where you need to look.

RESULTS

You might see a question that asks you to do the reverse of the above; that is, instead of asking what results come from new conditions, it'll ask which conditions would yield new results. The method for answering is the same: identify the relevant part of the passage (again, this is usually pretty easy—each experiment is set up to test a different variable, so look for the experiment that manipulates that variable), find the trend in the data, and use that trend to identify the conditions that will give you the desired result.

The bottom line with additional trials and experiments questions is that the answer is in the passage. Additional trials and experiments must conform to the data you've already been given. Be wary of answer choices that stray too far from the passage.

NEW INFORMATION

Sometimes, the questions following a Research Summaries passage will introduce new information. That information might come in the form of text in the question stem or a new table or graph. Your job with these questions is to figure out how this new information relates to what's already stated in the passage and find an answer choice that works with both the passage and the new information.

Questions with new information can be confusing on first read. One strategy is to save these questions for last. That gives you a chance to become more familiar with the data in the passage before you try to integrate additional data.

PRACTICE QUESTIONS

PASSAGE II

Before it can be considered safe to drink, water pumped from the ground or piped from an above-ground reservoir must be treated to remove contaminants. Suspended particles of organic and inorganic matter, parasites such as *Giardia*, bacteria, and toxic metal ions, especially lead (Pb), arsenic (As), and copper (Cu), must be removed for the water to be considered safe for consumption. Several methods of water filtration were investigated by scientists.

Method 1

Water was filtered through a rapid sand filter. The funnel-shaped filter is constructed from an upper layer of activated carbon and a thicker layer of sand below that, as shown in diagram 1. Particles too large to pass through the spaces between grains of sand are trapped in the upper layers of sand, and smaller particles are trapped in pore spaces or adhere to the sand. Rapid sand filters do not remove dissolved metal ions. The efficiency of particle removal was tested using filters of different depth. Data are shown in table 1.

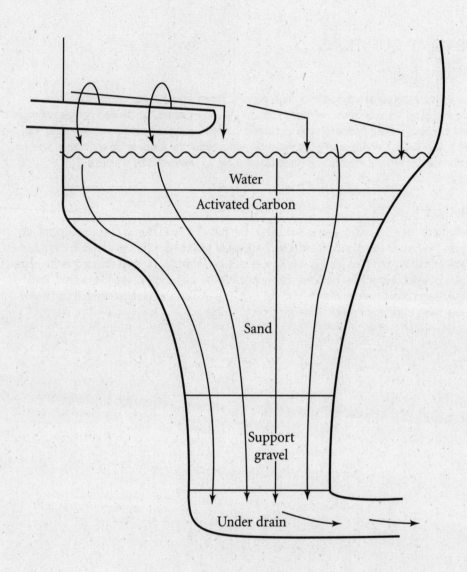

Table 1

Filter Depth (m)	Particles Removed (%)	Time for Filter Efficiency to Drop to 50% (hours)
0.6	95	2
0.8	98	3
1.0	99	4
1.2	99	5

Method 2

After filtering through the rapid sand filter, the water was pumped into storage tanks and treated with various concentrations of chlorine to destroy parasites and bacteria. Data are shown in table 2.

Table 2

Chlorine Concentration (parts per million)	Parasites and Bacteria Killed (%)
0.10	75
0.15	98
0.20	99.9
0.25	99.99
0.30	99.99

Method 3

The final step of water purification involves the removal of dangerous dissolved metal ions. To reduce these concentrations, a reverse osmosis filter was used (diagram 2). The size of the pores in the filter was varied, and the percentage of metal ions removed was calculated for each pore size. Data are shown in table 3.

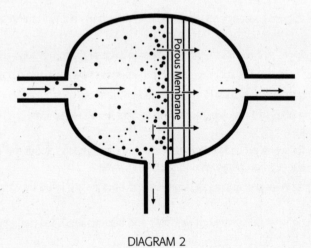

DIAGRAM 2

Table 3

Pore Size (angstroms)	As Removed (%)	Cu Removed (%)	Pb Removed (%)
2	62	78	85
3	59	77	98
4	51	68	92
5	47	62	84
6	30	56	70

1. How would the results of chlorinating water be affected, if at all, if excess chlorine-free water was accidentally added to the water in the chlorination tanks?

   A. The percentage of bacteria and parasites killed would decrease.

   B. The percentage of bacteria and parasites killed would increase.

   C. The percentage of bacteria and parasites killed would not change.

   D. The percentage of bacteria killed would increase while the percentage of parasites killed would decrease.

2. Which of the following statements about pore size is consistent with the results of Method 3?

   F. Increasing pore size results in an increased amount of Cu removed.

   G. Increasing pore size results in an increased amount of bacteria and parasites killed.

   H. Decreasing pore size results in an increased amount of As removed.

   J. Decreasing pore size requires more time to filter heavy metal ions.

3. Which of the following procedures would yield more information about the effects of chlorine concentration on parasites and bacteria in water?

   A. Determining what percentage of parasites and bacteria are killed by ultraviolet light exposure.

   B. Determining what percentage of parasites and bacteria are killed during the process of rapid sand filtering.

   C. Determining how the nutrient content of the water changes with chlorine concentration.

   D. Determining what percentages of individual types of parasites and bacteria are killed at different chlorine concentrations.

4. Scientists were concerned that sediment particles contained within the rapid sand filters were contributing to the amount of particles in the water exiting the filter. Which of the following procedures would best allow the scientists to investigate this issue?

   F. Filtering pure water through the filter and measuring the amount of particles in the water exiting the filter.

   G. Testing the amount of dissolved metal ions in the water before and after filtering.

   H. Adding additional sediment particles to the water before filtering.

   J. Measuring the amount of sediment in the water before and after filtering.

5. Over-chlorinating water can result in the production of potentially harmful chemical by-products called trihalomethanes (THMs). If chlorine concentrations above 0.25 parts per million (ppm) can result in dangerous levels of THMs in the water supply, which of the following chlorine concentrations should scientists recommend to safely purify drinking water of parasites and bacteria?

   A. 0.15 ppm

   B. 0.20 ppm

   C. 0.25 ppm

   D. 0.30 ppm

6. Molecules of zinc (Zn) are very close in size to molecules of Cu. If the percentage of Zn ions in water was also measured before and after reverse osmosis filtration, what relationship, if any, would scientists expect to see between pore size and percent Zn removal?

   F. As pore size increased, the percentage of Zn removed would increase.

   G. As pore size increased, the percentage of Zn removed would decrease.

   H. As pore size increased, the percentage of Zn removed would first increase, then decrease.

   J. As pore size increased, the percentage of Zn removed would first decrease, then increase.

7. If a city's water contained equal amounts of As, Cu, and Pb, a reverse osmosis filter with which pore size would remove the most heavy metals?

   A. 2 angstroms

   B. 3 angstroms

   C. 4 angstroms

   D. 5 angstroms

ANSWERS AND EXPLANATIONS

1. A

You're asked to predict how the accidental addition of chlorine-free water would effect the results obtained in Method 2. To answer, consider the relationship between the chlorine concentration and the percentage of bacteria and parasites killed. A quick glance back at table 2 clearly shows that as chlorine concentration increases, the percentage of bacteria and parasites killed also increases.

What, then, will happen to the concentration of chlorine in the water if chlorine-free water is introduced? Chlorine-free water would dilute the concentration of chlorine. This decrease in concentration would decrease the percentage of bacteria and parasites killed, so choice (A) is correct.

2. H

Remember that some Research Summaries questions will ask us to evaluate the experimental results, just like Data Representation questions. Here, we're asked to examine the relationship between pore size and heavy metal removal.

Begin by looking back over table 3. For both As and Cu, an increase in pore size results in a decrease in the percentage of heavy metal removed. For Pb, percentage removed increases when pore size is increased from two to three angstroms, and then decreases as pore size increases further.

Only choice (H) gets the relationship right (though the wording is a bit confusing—"decreasing" pore size means you have to read the table from bottom to top, which isn't how one usually approaches a table). Note that choices (G) and (J) don't relate to Method 3 at all, and that choice (F) gets the relationship backward.

3. D

The effect of chlorine concentration on parasites and bacteria was examined in Method 2. Further investigations about chlorine concentration should test something not already studied in Method 2. Only choice (D) identifies an experiment that would give us additional information about the effects of chlorine concentration on parasites and bacteria; it suggests finding out how specific kinds of parasites and bacteria each respond to chlorine concentration.

Choices (A) and (B) are incorrect because they do not offer any additional information about how *chlorine concentration* effects parasites and bacteria. Choice (C) is incorrect because we're asked to find out more about the effects of chlorine concentration on parasites and bacteria, not nutrient content.

4. F

The question stem tells us that the scientists are concerned that sediment contained within the rapid sand filter itself is contributing to the amount of particles in the water exiting the filter. To test whether this is an issue, it would make sense for the scientists to run pure, particle-free water through the filter and see if any sediment particles are contained in the water exiting the filter, as in choice (F).

Choice (G) is irrelevant to the issue of particles within the filter. Heavy metal ions are discussed in Method 3, but have no bearing on the particle-removing rapid sand filters discussed in Method 1.

Choice (H) is also incorrect. Adding additional sediment to the water before filtering won't tell scientists anything about whether the filter itself is adding particles to the water. Choice (J) is likewise incorrect. The amount of sediment in the water is already being measured before and after filtering, to determine the percentage of sediment removed by each filter. It offers us no additional information.

5. C

Many questions on the ACT Science Test will introduce some additional information, either in the form of information within the question stem, as is the case here, or in the form of additional tables or graphs. Our task in this situation is to integrate this new information with the information already in the passage.

To answer this question, we must look back at table 2. It shows that chlorine concentrations of 0.10 ppm kill 75% of parasites and bacteria, concentrations of 0.15 ppm kill 98% of parasites and bacteria, concentrations of 0.20 ppm kill 99.9% of parasites and bacteria, and concentrations of 0.25 ppm and higher kill 99.99% of parasites and bacteria. The question stem, however, tells us that concentrations *over* 0.25 ppm result in dangerously high THM levels. Scientists should, then, recommend that water be treated with the lowest chlorine concentration that still kills the highest percentage of parasites and bacteria. That would be 0.25 ppm, as in choice (C).

6. G

Here we are asked to predict the results of an additional measurement in an experiment. Scientists didn't measure the percentage of zinc removed by reverse osmosis filtration. However, we're told in the question stem that zinc molecules are about the same size as copper molecules. Table 3 shows us that pore size is directly related to the percentage of each metal that is removed. We can infer, then, that if zinc is about the same size as copper, it'll be removed by the reverse osmosis filter similarly to copper.

How is the percentage of copper removed related to pore size? We should resist the temptation to speed through this question by answering from memory. It only takes a few more seconds to double-check the table!

A quick scan down the Cu column shows us that as pore size increases, the percentage of copper removed decreases. This matches choice (G).

7. B

This question asks us to determine which set of experimental conditions gives us a specified result. In this case, the specified result is the greatest amount of heavy metals removed.

To investigate, we should look back to table 3. It shows that as pore size increases, the percent of As and Cu removed decreases. However, notice that Pb doesn't exactly follow this trend. At 2 angstroms, 85% of Pb is removed. But at 3 angstroms, 98% of Pb is removed. That's a different trend, and underscores the importance of evaluating *all* of the data before answering a question. Once pore size is increased over 3 angstroms, the percentage of Pb removed sharply plummets.

To determine whether 2 angstroms or 3 angstroms is the best answer, we must evaluate, approximately, which size results in more total metal removed. We're told that the city's water contains equal amounts of As, Cu, and Pb. The decrease in the percent of As and Cu removed when pore size is increased from 2 to 3 angstroms is tiny (3% and 1% respectively), but the increase in Pb removed is significant (13%). We don't need a calculator (and aren't allowed one anyway!) to realize that more metal is removed at 3 angstroms than at 2 angstroms. Choice (B) is correct.

Chapter Seventeen: **Research Summaries III**

The final set of skills you'll need to attack Research Summaries passages with confidence is the ability to understand complex experiments, to understand the hypothesis for an experiment, and to integrate new, complex information into the information already given in the passage. The good news about complex Research Summaries passages is that the ACT likes to keep passages at approximately the same level of difficulty. That means that complicated passages will usually be balanced with simpler questions. So don't let all of the complicated-looking diagrams and apparatus scare you off!

UNDERSTANDING COMPLEX EXPERIMENTS

You'll be able to recognize a complex Research Summaries passage instantly: They're the ones with scary-looking diagrams of experimental apparatus, lots of text, and a combination of tables and graphs (just one type of data presentation would be too simple!) The multiple experiments will probably be quite different from each other, which is a big contrast to the simpler Research Summaries passages. Simple passages usually contain experiments that are very similar variations of each other, changing just one variable at a time and using the same experimental design.

If you get a really complex Research Summaries passage on your ACT, read carefully through it one time but do not get bogged down in the details. Remember, you don't get points for understanding the passage, just for answering questions (correctly, of course!). Stay focused. Don't let your mind wander as you're reading, but don't worry about the details until a question sends you there.

The same goes for the complex apparatus diagrams. On your first read, note their existence. You can puzzle them out in detail when (or if) a question directs you to.

Finally, treat a complex data presentation like a combination of simpler ones. Look carefully for the variable in question (search for the appropriate units if you're having trouble finding it) and identify the trends in the data. The information you need is there, but it's surrounded by data you don't need. Work methodically and you won't be thrown by it.

UNDERSTANDING HYPOTHESES

While you'll likely never be asked to directly identify the hypothesis for an experiment, the ACT does test your understanding of hypotheses in general. So what is a hypothesis? It's the scientists' guess at the answer to the question they're asking (reread chapter 11 for more on hypotheses and the scientific method in general).

Usually, the ACT makes it pretty clear when they're giving you a hypothesis, so you don't have to worry about ever coming up with one on your own. You'll see dead giveaways when you're dealing with a hypothesis question, like "If Scientist 1's hypothesis is correct…" You do need to understand how to support or weaken that hypothesis, or how to further test it.

Supporting a hypothesis means backing it up with more information that fits the hypothesis. Weakening it means finding information that contradicts the hypothesis. To further test a hypothesis, you'll need to ask yourself what else you need to know to confirm or disprove this guess.

NEW INFORMATION

As you may recall from chapter 16, you should be prepared for questions that introduce new information, be it in the form of text, graphs, tables, or diagrams. Your job on these questions is to find an answer choice that combines both the new information and the information already presented in the passage. Questions that introduce new information are generally not as hard as they seem, but can be time consuming. It's a good idea to save these for last.

PRACTICE QUESTIONS

PASSAGE III

The *reaction rate* of a chemical reaction is defined as how quickly the reaction takes place. Students wished to investigate the reaction rate, burn time, and peak burn temperature for three common combustion reactions.

Study 1

Students used a computer model to simulate the combustion of pure hydrogen (H_2), methane (CH_4), and propane (C_3H_8). The model was created with the assumption that the reactions took place in a closed system of constant volume. Figure 1 shows the computer-generated reaction rates as a function of temperature for hydrogen, methane, and propane gas.

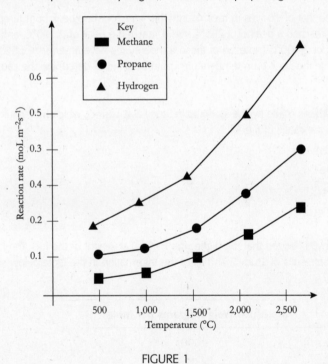

FIGURE 1

Study 2

Students next measured the *burn time* (the length of time for which a fixed amount of each fuel will burn), *ignition temperature* (the temperature at which the fuel spontaneously ignites), and the peak temperature of each fuel by igniting a fixed amount of each fuel and a fixed amount of air inside a closed, heatproof, insulated container. A *thermocouple* (high temperature electronic thermometer) was affixed to the container to measure temperature. Their results are shown in table 1 below.

Table 1

Fuel	Amount (g)	Burn Time (s)	Ignition Temperature (°C)	Peak Temperature (°C)
Hydrogen	0.1	103	585	2,318
Propane	0.1	256	487	2,385
Methane	0.1	321	540	2,148

Study 3

Students learned that of 10 fires in their county this year, four had peak burn temperatures over 1,500°C: fire 1 reached a peak of 2,295°C, fire 4 reached a peak of 2,100°C, and fires 5 and 9 reached a peak of 2,400°C (note: all of these temperatures have an error of ±50°C). Students hypothesized that the peak burn temperature could be used to determine the cause of these fires.

1. If the hypothesis made by the students in Study 3 is correct, which fuel would most likely have been the cause of fire 9?

    A. Hydrogen
    B. Methane
    C. Propane
    D. Kerosene

2. A student hypothesized that the higher the molecular weight of the fuel, the longer its burn time. Do the results of Study 2 and all of the information in the table below support this hypothesis?

Gas	Molecular Weight (grams per mole)
Hydrogen	1.008
Propane	44.096
Methane	16.043

    F. Yes; propane has the highest molecular weight of the gasses and the longest burn time.
    G. Yes; propane has a higher molecular weight than hydrogen and a longer burn time.
    H. No; the higher the molecular weight of a fuel, the shorter its burn time.
    J. No; there is no clear relationship between molecular weight and burn time.

3. A student hypothesized that increasing the pressure on a fuel would increase its reaction rate. The best way to verify this hypothesis would be to repeat Study 1 with:

   A. changing pressures instead of changing temperatures.

   B. higher temperatures.

   C. different fuels.

   D. greater initial amounts of the fuels.

4. According to Study 1, which of the following statements best describes the relationship, if any, between temperature and reaction rate?

   F. As temperature increases, reaction rate increases.

   G. As temperature increases, reaction rate decreases.

   H. As temperature increases, reaction rate first increases, then decreases.

   J. There is no apparent relationship between temperature and reaction rate.

5. Which of the following graphs best represents the relationship between the ignition temperature and burn time of the three fuels?

A.

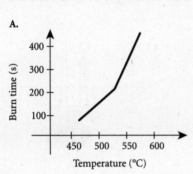

B.

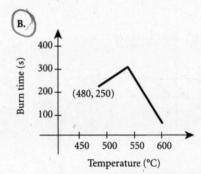

C.

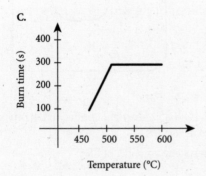

D.

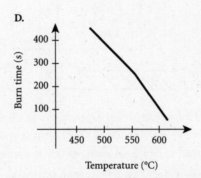

6. Which of the following figures best illustrates the apparatus described in Study 2?

F.

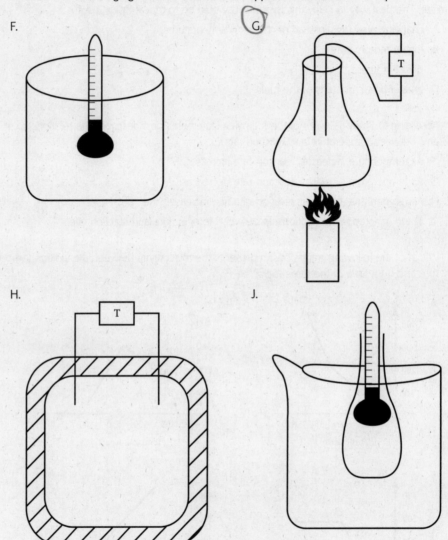

G.

H.

J.

7. Which of the following best explains why students used a fixed amount of fuel to determine burn times in Study 2? The students wanted to be certain that:

A. variations in burn time were not due to varying starting amounts of fuel.

B. the fuel had enough time to burn completely.

C. the temperature in the container was hot enough to ignite the fuel.

D. no other fuels were present in the container.

ANSWERS AND EXPLANATIONS

1. C

To answer this question, we must first determine exactly what hypothesis the students made in Study 3. Going back to the passage, we see that "Students hypothesized that the peak burn temperature could be used to determine the cause of these fires." In other words, the students believed that the peak burn temperature of the fire would correlate to the peak burn temperature of the fuel that caused it. The question becomes, what was the peak temperature of fire 9, and which fuel has a peak burn temperature closest to that?

According to Study 3, the peak temperature of fire 9 was 2,400°C, plus or minus 50°C. We can find peak burn temperatures for each fuel in table 1. According to the table, the only fuel with a peak burn temperature in the range of 2,350°C to 2,450°C is propane, with a peak burn temperature of 2,385°C. The correct answer is choice (C).

Note that you could certainly have eliminated choice (D)—nowhere in the passage is kerosene mentioned, so it cannot possibly be correct.

2. J

This is a rather complex question. It requires us to combine information from two sources to come up with an answer. Remember, though, that complex doesn't have to mean difficult. Even the most complex questions usually break down into a series of simpler steps. Your job is to keep your cool and work methodically, one step at a time.

The first step is to understand the hypothesis presented in the question stem. A student is saying that higher molecular weights of fuels mean longer burn times. It's a good idea to underline that first sentence, or at least circle the words "higher molecular weight" and "longer burn time," to avoid making a simple error.

Molecular weight isn't mentioned anywhere in the passage, but this missing information is printed in a table for us just below the question stem. It shows that hydrogen has the lowest molecular weight, followed by methane, then propane. Because the fuels aren't listed in increasing or decreasing order of molecular weight, it's a good idea

to jot "hydrogen, methane, propane" (the fuels in order of increasing molecular weight) down next to the table, to avoid confusion.

Next, we have to order the fuels according to burn time. According to table 1, hydrogen has the shortest burn time, then propane, then methane. Finally, we can determine whether a higher molecular weight means a longer burn time. It doesn't. While hydrogen has the shortest burn time and lowest molecular weight, the pattern breaks with propane and methane. The correct answer, then, is choice (J).

While it's true that propane has a higher molecular weight than hydrogen and a longer burn time, as in choice (G), that's not enough to make the entire hypothesis true, so choice (G) is incorrect.

3. A

To verify a hypothesis, we need data. To acquire this data, the student would have to modify Study 1 so that it provided information about the effects of pressure on reaction rate. Only choice (A) mentions pressure, and it is correct.

Choice (B) is incorrect. If Study 1 were repeated with higher temperatures, we'd learn more about the effect of temperature on reaction rate, but nothing about pressure. Since the question stem asks us to verify a hypothesis concerning the effects of pressure on reaction rate, the correct answer choice must incorporate pressure.

Choices (C) and (D) are again incorrect because they don't test pressure. Repeating the study with different fuels, or differing initial amounts of fuel, would tell us nothing about pressure and reaction rate.

4. F

To find the relationship between temperature and reaction rate, we need to look back to figure 1. Temperature is given on the x-axis, and reaction rate on the y-axis. Temperature is increasing left to right from 500°C to 2,500°C, and reaction rate increases from 0.1 to 0.6 as you move up. Now, look at the shape of the curve itself; it points up. This means that as temperature increases, the reaction rate increases. Choice (F) is correct.

Note that choice (G) states the opposite relationship, and choice (H) gives a relationship that is more complicated than the one shown by the figure. If the reaction rate first increased, then decreased, we'd expect to see a curve that looks like a hill—going up and then going back down. That's not what figure 1 shows.

5.   B

Here's an example of a question that asks us to plot the relationship between two variables. We first covered these kinds of questions in chapter 13 (look back to the section titled "Translating Information into a Table, Graph, or Diagram" for a quick review). These kinds of questions can appear anywhere in the Science Test, even on the Conflicting Viewpoints passage.

Remember, we don't actually have to generate our own plot here, just pick the correct one from the four answer choices. So, what should the correct plot look like?

The correct plot should list ignition temperature in degrees Celsius on the *x*-axis and burn time in seconds on the *y*-axis. It should also plot the values shown in table 1: Propane's ignition temperature is 487°C and its burn time is 256 seconds; methane's ignition temperature is 540°C and its burn time is 321 seconds; and hydrogen's ignition temperature is 585°C and its burn time is 103 seconds.

Only the graph shown in choice (B) correctly plots these values, so it is correct.

6.   H

Study 2 explains the experimental setup by stating that students ignited "a fixed amount of each fuel and a fixed amount of air inside a closed, heatproof, insulated container. A *thermocouple* (high temperature electronic thermometer) was affixed to the container to measure temperature."

We need an answer choice that shows a closed, heatproof container containing fuel and air, with a thermocouple affixed. Only choice (H) comes close, and it is correct.

Choice (F) is incorrect because it shows the ignition taking place in an open container. Furthermore, it shows a standard thermometer inside the container, which contradicts the explanation given.

Choice (G) is incorrect because it shows a flask held over a Bunsen burner, which likewise contradicts the given explanation.

Choice (J) is incorrect because it shows a flask with a standard thermometer inside another flask, which again contradicts the given explanation.

7.   A

Here is a question that requires us to understand the methods of a complex experiment. What was the purpose of using a fixed amount of fuel in determining burn time?

Usually, the easiest way to deal with "which of the following" kinds of questions is to go straight to the answer choices. Of course, if the correct answer pops into your head first, even better. But failing that, it's generally fastest to scan the answer choices for the correct answer.

Choice (A) states the students wanted to be certain that "variations in burn time were not due to varying starting amounts of fuel." This is certainly true—it's reasonable to assume that the more fuel you start with, the longer it will burn. So, if we're going to compare burn times directly, we have to be certain we're controlling all of the other variables. Let's just check the other choices to be certain we have the correct one.

Choice (B) states the students wanted to be certain that "the fuel had enough time to burn completely." This doesn't make sense. Students were measuring the burn time, but using equal amounts of starting fuel each time wouldn't help students be certain that they had allowed the fuel to burn completely. Cross this one off.

Choice (C) states the students wanted to be certain that "the temperature in the container was hot enough to ignite the fuel." This likewise doesn't make sense. There's no connection between ignition temperature and using equal starting amounts of fuel. Cross this one off, too.

Choice (D) states the students wanted to be certain that "no other fuels were present in the container." While students would certainly want to be sure they were burning one fuel at a time when measuring burn times, using fixed amounts of each fuel wouldn't accomplish this. Cross it off.

Choice (A), then, is correct.

Chapter Eighteen: **Conflicting Viewpoints I**

Conflicting Viewpoints passages are a bit of an oddball in the ACT Science Test. While there are three each of Data Representation and Research Summaries passages, you'll have just one Conflicting Viewpoints passage. And while Data Representation and Research Summaries passages present information from one or more experiments, Conflicting Viewpoints passages by and large contain only some opening information and the viewpoints of two, three, or four authors. They are far less likely to contain any figures (although it does happen), and resemble ACT Reading Test passages as much as they do Science passages.

Conflicting Viewpoints passages focus on a different set of skills than Data Representation and Research Summaries passages. While the latter test your ability to locate and analyze data, Conflicting Viewpoints passages primarily test your ability to understand a hypothesis (you can consider each viewpoint to be one author's hypothesis). They'll also test your ability to determine whether additional information would support or weaken a viewpoint and to identify similarities and differences between the viewpoints.

UNDERSTANDING THE VIEWPOINTS

Some of the questions that accompany a Conflicting Viewpoints passage will simply test your ability to identify key issues or assumptions in each viewpoint. They're typically rather straightforward, and reliably contain wrong answer choices that draw from other viewpoints to trick you into getting the question wrong. That's why it's important to follow the Kaplan Method for Conflicting Viewpoints passages, which was introduced in chapter 11.

The Kaplan Method for Conflicting Viewpoints Passages

1. Read the introductory text and the first author's viewpoint, then answer the questions that ask only about the first author's viewpoint.
2. Read the second author's viewpoint, then answer the questions that ask only about the second author's viewpoint.
3. Answer the questions that refer to both authors' viewpoints.

This will require that you skip around in the questions. That's fine. There's no rule saying you have to answer the questions in the order in which they appear. And you'll find that it's much,

much easier to deal with Conflicting Viewpoints passages when you minimize your opportunities to confuse the two (or three, or four) viewpoints.

SUPPORTING AND WEAKENING VIEWPOINTS

While there are no guarantees on the ACT, it's common to see at least one question asking you to identify whether information supports or weakens the view of one or both authors. Typically, these questions will introduce new information or data, and your job will be to determine whether the data supports or weakens a viewpoint.

Remember that information supports a viewpoint if it offers data that makes the viewpoint even more likely to be true. Conversely, information weakens a viewpoint if it contradicts some part of it. The information doesn't have to prove a viewpoint to be true in order to support it, and it doesn't have to prove it false to weaken it. You're simply supposed to judge whether the information adds to or detracts from any part of the viewpoint.

IDENTIFYING SIMILARITIES AND DIFFERENCES BETWEEN VIEWPOINTS

You might see questions that ask you to identify a point on which the authors agree, or a point on which they disagree. It's helpful in answering these questions to underline each author's main point as you're reading. Then, when it's time to identify similarities and differences, you'll have the essence of their viewpoints highlighted.

Answer these questions immediately after you answer the questions that deal with just one viewpoint at a time. Questions that ask you to identify similarities or differences are typically among the easier questions in the passage, so they're great for giving you a chance to make sure you have the subtleties of each viewpoint nailed down.

PRACTICE QUESTIONS

PASSAGE I

Acids are chemical compounds that are today most fundamentally defined as having a pH less than 7.0—that is, a hydrogen ion activity greater than pure water—when dissolved in water and which are capable of donating a proton. Bases are chemical compounds with a pH higher than 7.0 and are commonly understood as compounds that can accept protons. Before chemists developed the modern model of acid and base behavior, there were many attempts to explain their observable qualities; especially the observable qualities of acids (sour taste, an ability to turn blue vegetable dye red, an ability to conduct an electric current, and, most notably, an ability to react with certain compounds and give off hydrogen or carbon dioxide gas). Two historical definitions of acids are presented below.

Lavoisier Definition

Lavoisier believed that all acids showed the same observable properties because they contained one common substance. Because he primarily knew of strong acids such as HNO_3 and H_2SO_4, he believed that this common substance was oxygen (O). He believed that a metal, reacting with an acid, would combine with the oxygen in the acid to produce a *calx* (a metal oxide). The calx would then further react with the acid to form a salt. Hydrogen, the other component of water, was released as a gas. The reaction could also run in reverse. Water, combined with a salt and calx, would produce an acid. Oxygen, according to Lavoisier, was the driving force behind the reaction. In fact, Lavoisier himself actually recognized and named the element oxygen, deriving the word from the Greek for "acid-producer."

Lavoisier further believed that the other portions of the acidic compound were responsible for the acid's specific individual properties, and called this other portion the "acidifiable base." He had no further understanding of bases.

Liebig Definition

Liebig primarily studied organic acids such as CH_3COOH (acetic acid) and $C_3H_6O_3$ (lactic acid). According to the Liebig definition, it was not oxygen but rather hydrogen (H) that was responsible for the common properties of an acid. However, not all compounds containing hydrogen could be considered acidic; Liebig defined an acid as a hydrogen-containing compound in which the hydrogen could be replaced by a metal. The hydrogen would then be released as a gas. Liebig recognized a base as a substance capable of *neutralizing* an acid (neutralization is the process by which an acid is transformed into a salt and water and no longer displays the common characteristics of an acid), but had no theoretical understanding of how and why bases worked.

1. Which of the following assumptions was made by Lavoisier?

    A. All acids combine with oxygen as they react.

    B. Acids cannot be broken down into other compounds.

    C. All acids contain oxygen.

    D. Any compound that contains oxygen is an acid.

2. Adherents of which definition, if either, would predict that hydrochloric acid (HCl) has a pH of less than 7?

   F. The Lavoisier definition only
   G. The Liebig definition only
   H. Both the Lavoisier definition and the Liebig definition
   J. Neither the Lavoisier definition nor the Liebig definition

3. According to the Lavoisier definition, the combination of a salt, hydrogen gas, and metal oxide would produce a:

   A. calx.
   B. neutral salt.
   C. base.
   D. acid.

4. According to the Liebig definition of acids, the gas produced from the reaction of an acid:

   F. is heavier than air.
   G. is composed of hydrogen.
   H. is suitable for breathing.
   J. is composed of oxygen.

5. When phosphoric acid (H_3PO_4) reacts with sodium bromide (NaBr), monosodium phosphate (NaH_2PO_4) and hydrobromic acid (HBr) are produced according to the equation $NaBr + H_3PO_4 \rightarrow NaH_2PO_4 + HBr$. What conclusion would adherents of each definition draw about the mechanics of this reaction?

   A. Both adherents of the Lavoisier definition and adherents of the Liebig definition would conclude that the reaction is driven by the oxygen contained in the phosphoric acid.
   B. Both adherents of the Lavoisier definition and adherents of the Liebig definition would conclude that the reaction is driven by the hydrogen contained in the phosphoric acid.
   C. Adherents of the Lavoisier definition would conclude that the reaction is driven by the oxygen contained in the phosphoric acid; adherents of the Liebig definition would conclude that the reaction is driven by the hydrogen contained in the phosphoric acid.
   D. Adherents of the Lavoisier definition would conclude that the reaction is driven by the hydrogen contained in the phosphoric acid; adherents of the Liebig definition would conclude that the reaction is driven by the oxygen contained in the phosphoric acid.

NO

6. Suppose an acid is allowed to react completely with a metal. Which of the following statements about acids is most consistent with the information presented in the passage?

    F. If the Lavoisier definition is correct, the oxygen in the acid will have donated a proton in the reaction.

    G. If the Lavoisier definition is correct, the hydrogen in the acid will have accepted a proton in the reaction.

    H. If the Liebig definition is correct, the oxygen in the acid will have donated a proton in the reaction.

    J. If the Liebig definition is correct, the hydrogen in the acid will have accepted a proton in the reaction.

7. The Liebig definition states that the hydrogen in an acid is capable of being replaced by a metal. Which of the following findings, if true, could be used to *counter* this definition?

    A. Acids, when reacted, release pure hydrogen gas.

    B. Acids, when neutralized, form solutions with a pH equal to that of pure water.

    C. In the reaction of sulfuric acid (H_2SO_4) with sodium hydroxide (NaOH), sodium sulfate (Na_2SO_4) and water are formed.

    D. Some acids, when completely reacted, form pure metals in water.

8. The Lavoisier definition differs from the Liebig definition in that only the Liebig definition states that a base:

    F. is capable of neutralizing an acid.

    G. has a pH of greater than 7.

    H. is responsible for an acid's specific qualities.

    J. could be formed by combining a calx with a metal oxide.

KAPLAN

ANSWERS AND EXPLANATIONS

1. C

The passage states that "Lavoisier believed that all acids showed the same observable properties because they contained one common substance." In the next sentence, the passage goes on to state that "he believed that this common substance was oxygen (O)." So according to Lavoisier, all acids contain one common substance, and that substance is oxygen. Choice (C) is correct.

Choice (A) is incorrect because it very subtly twists the relationship in the passage. Acids don't *combine* with oxygen, they actually *contain* oxygen. If we were to rush through this question because it looks pretty easy, we might fall into this wrong answer trap.

Choice (B) is incorrect. The Lavoisier definition never states that acids cannot be broken down into other compounds. Quite the opposite—the definition states that acids can react with metals to produce hydrogen gas and a salt.

Choice (D) is incorrect because it also subtly twists the definition given in the passage. The Lavoisier definition states that all acids contain oxygen, but we cannot conclude from this statement that all compounds containing oxygen are acids.

2. G

The opening paragraph states that "Acids are chemical compounds that are today most fundamentally defined as having a pH less than 7.0". So this question stem is really asking us to decide who would predict that HCl is an acid.

According to the Lavoisier definition, all acids contain oxygen (O). According to the Liebig definition, all acids contain hydrogen (H). Hydrochloric acid, which contains hydrogen and not oxygen, would only be expected to be an acid according to the Liebig definition. Choice (G) is correct.

3. D

Go back to the passage to answer this question. The details about how salts, gasses, and metal oxides react in this definition are too complicated to recall off the top of your head. The Lavoisier definition states in the first paragraph that Lavoisier, "believed that a metal, reacting with

an acid, would combine with the oxygen in the acid to produce a *calx* (a metal oxide). The calx would then further react with the acid to form a salt. Hydrogen, the other component of water, was released as a gas. The reaction could also run in reverse. Water, combined with a salt and calx, would produce an acid."

Let's work slowly. The question stem is asking us about the combination of a salt, hydrogen gas, and metal oxide. The first two sentences that we quoted above tell us about how an acid can break a metal down into a salt and hydrogen gas (a component of water). The last sentence tells us that the reaction also works in reverse—water can combine with a salt and calx to produce an acid. The question stem asks us what will happen when we combine hydrogen gas with a salt and a metal oxide. The passage tells us that hydrogen gas is a component of water, and a metal oxide is also known as calx. So the question stem is merely asking us in other terms what happens when we combine water with a salt and a calx. According to the last sentence we quoted, the answer is an acid. Choice (D) is correct.

4. G

We should approach this question by making sure we understand exactly what the Liebig definition says about the gas produced from the reaction of an acid. Back to the passage!

The passage states that "Liebig defined an acid as a hydrogen-containing compound in which the hydrogen could be replaced by a metal. The hydrogen could then be released as a gas." So we need to look for an answer choice that matches this statement. Choice (G) fits best.

Choice (F) is incorrect. The passage doesn't say anything about whether hydrogen gas is flammable (it is, though).

Choice (H) is also incorrect; hydrogen gas is not suitable for breathing. No gas's suitability is mentioned in the passage, so we can eliminate this answer choice anyway. Very rarely will questions rely on your knowledge of basic science facts, but it does happen. The ACT very occasionally assumes that we know things like which gases are safe for breathing.

Choice (J) is incorrect. The Liebig definition does not state that oxygen is given off when an acid is reacted.

5. C

This question manages to make a very simple idea look extraordinarily complicated. By working methodically and not panicking, we'll see that getting to the answer is far easier than it first appears.

The question stem gives us the equation for a reaction between an acid (H_3PO_4) and a metal (NaBr). We're asked to decide who would conclude what based on this reaction.

Let's make sure we understand exactly what each definition states. According to the Lavoisier definition, acids are acids because they contain oxygen. According to the Liebig definition, acids are acids because they contain hydrogen. Since H_3PO_4 contains both hydrogen and oxygen, we can expect that adherents of the Lavoisier definition would conclude that the oxygen in H_3PO_4 is responsible for the reaction, while adherents of the Liebig definition would conclude that the hydrogen is responsible for the reaction. This matches choice (C).

Note that choice (D) gets the definitions backward, and is therefore incorrect.

6. F

This question requires us to combine information in the passage with information in the question stem to support one of the viewpoints. As is typical with "which of the following" type questions, it's easiest to begin this one by moving straight to the answer choices.

Choice (F) reads "If the Lavoisier definition is correct, the oxygen in the acid will have donated a proton in the reaction." To know whether this is true, we need to know what the passage says about protons. That information appears in the opening paragraph. The first sentence says that "Acids are chemical compounds…capable of donating a proton." So, if acids donate protons, and a hypothetical acid has reacted with a metal, is it consistent with the Lavoisier definition to state that the oxygen in the acid donated a proton? Yes. The Lavoisier definition maintains that oxygen is the component of an acid responsible for the characteristic behavior of an acid. Therefore, if the definition is correct, then the oxygen will have donated the proton.

Note that choice (G) makes two mistakes. It attributes the acid-like behavior to the hydrogen in the acid, which is consistent with the Liebig definition and not the Lavoisier definition, and it states that the acid will have *accepted* a proton, which, according to the passage, is characteristic of a base, not an acid.

Choices (H) and (J) similarly confuse the main tenets of each definition and the definitions of an acid and a base given in the first paragraph.

7. D

To counter an argument means to go against it. So, we're looking for the finding that contradicts Liebig's definition. This is a "which of the following" question, so we should go straight to evaluating the answer choices.

Choice (A) states that "Acids, when reacted, release pure hydrogen gas." Does this contradict the idea that the hydrogen in an acid is capable of being replaced by a metal? No. If anything, it strengthens it, because it supports the idea that the hydrogen in an acid is released (though it doesn't speak to what that hydrogen might be replaced by). Eliminate this one.

Choice (B) states that "Acids, when neutralized, form solutions with a pH equal to that of pure water." Does this counter the given definition of acids? No. The pH of neutralized acids doesn't tell us whether the hydrogen has been replaced by a metal. Eliminate it.

Choice (C) gives us the reaction of sulfuric acid and sodium hydroxide. The product is sodium sulfate. This reaction supports the Liebig definition; the hydrogen in the acid has been replaced in the final product by a metal (Na). This supports the Liebig definition, so it is certainly not correct.

Choice (D) states that "Some acids, when completely reacted, form pure metals in water." This would counter the Liebig definition. The hydrogen in an acid can't be replaced by a metal if pure metals in water are formed. It is correct.

8. F

Here's another question asking us to identify one difference between the definitions. This is the first question in the passage to ask us about a base, so we should make sure we understand what each definition states about them.

According to the first viewpoint, Lavoisier believed that "the other portions of the acidic compound were responsible for the acid's specific individual properties, and called this other portion the 'acidifiable base.'"

According to the second viewpoint, Liebig believed that a base was "a substance capable of neutralizing an acid." This matches choice (F) perfectly, and it is correct.

Note that choice (G) pulls from the introductory material. This is tricky because while it is true, it's not specific to the Liebig definition. Choice (H) is incorrect because it matches the Lavoisier definition of bases. While choice (J) might be tempting because it uses terms from the passage, there is nothing in the Liebig definition to suggest how a base might be formed.

Chapter Nineteen: **Conflicting Viewpoints II**

Even though you'll see just one Conflicting Viewpoints passage on your ACT Science Test, as opposed to three each of Data Representation and Research Summaries passages, the questions that might accompany your Conflicting Viewpoints passage are as varied as those that might accompany the other two passage types. Some Conflicting Viewpoints passages and their questions are more technical, focusing on the mechanics of a specific scientific question (like the passage that accompanies this chapter), while others are more theoretical (like the passages that accompany chapters 18 and 20). You should practice with a variety of Conflicting Viewpoints passages so you'll be prepared for whatever passage you get.

Some passages will contain many questions focused on strengthening and weakening the viewpoints. These questions will incorporate a lot of new information in the question stems. Some questions might ask you to make predictions about seemingly unrelated subjects based on the viewpoints, and some might ask you to find hypotheses, conclusions, or predictions that are supported by two viewpoints or pieces of information.

MORE ON STRENGTHENING AND WEAKENING VIEWPOINTS

You might see questions that introduce new information, and then ask you whether this information supports or weakens one or both viewpoints. Some questions might even ask you *why* the information supports or weakens a viewpoint.

The questions that introduce new information sometimes look really confusing. The information might look overly complex, or appear at first to have nothing to do with the rest of the passage. Remember that the questions don't rely on any outside knowledge, so you *do* have the information you need to answer them. Break these questions down into a series of simple steps, and always start by making sure you understand each viewpoint. Remember that information supports a viewpoint if it makes it more likely to be true, and weakens it if it makes the viewpoint less likely to be true.

MAKING PREDICTIONS BASED ON VIEWPOINTS

Questions that ask you to make predictions based on the viewpoints are especially common with the more technical passages. These questions often require you to apply a viewpoint to a specific process, or a hypothetical situation, and make a prediction about the outcome. For example, one recent ACT Conflicting Viewpoints passage presented four viewpoints about gene replication in bacteria. The questions accompanying this passage were focused almost exclusively on predicting the order in which the genes would be copied according to each viewpoint.

Confusion is the biggest source of error in these situations. Make sure you minimize potential confusion by reading one viewpoint at a time, and then answering the questions that apply to just that viewpoint.

HYPOTHESES, CONCLUSIONS, AND PREDICTIONS SUPPORTED BY TWO VIEWPOINTS

Another complicated question type will ask you to find hypotheses, conclusions, and predictions that are supported by two or more viewpoints or pieces of information. Again, your job is to find an answer choice that is compatible with both viewpoints, or with one viewpoint and some additional information. Make sure you understand exactly what each viewpoint states, or how the viewpoint in question relates to the additional information in the question stem, before you answer the question. A big source of error on the ACT Science Test is moving to the answer choices before you know what you're looking for. Make sure you have a guess in mind before reading the answer choices. For questions that ask "which of the following…", it's generally quicker to evaluate the answer choices without making a guess, but you need to be certain that you know how to tell whether each choice is correct before you start.

PRACTICE QUESTIONS

PASSAGE II

The *molecular geometry* of a molecule is the three-dimensional appearance of that molecule. Molecular geometry determines many of the properties of a substance, most notably its phase of matter, reactivity, polarity, and magnetism. While molecular geometries can be determined absolutely through X-ray crystallography or quantum mechanical modeling, they can also be predicted with the *valence shell electron-pair repulsion* (VSEPR) theory.

The VSEPR theory uses Lewis structures (diagrams that show the bonding between atoms and lone electron pairs in a molecule) to predict the molecular geometry of covalently bonded molecules. VSEPR theory states that the shape of a molecule is determined by the repulsions between the bonded and nonbonded pairs of electrons in the outer shell of the molecule's central atom. These electron pairs arrange themselves as far apart as possible to minimize repulsion.

There are five basic molecular geometries:

1. *Linear.* In a linear molecule, two electron pairs are arranged in a line around a central atom. The bond angle between the electron pairs is 180°.
2. *Trigonal planar.* A molecule with trigonal planar geometry has three electron pairs arranged around a central atom, with a bond angle of 120° between electron pairs.
3. *Tetrahedral.* In a molecule with tetrahedral geometry, the central atom is surrounded by four electron pairs, each with bond angles of 109.5°.
4. *Trigonal bipyramidal.* Molecules with this geometry contain five electron pairs. The bond angles are 90°, 120°, and 180°.
5. *Octahedral.* Molecules with octahedral geometry contain six electron pairs around one central atom. Bond angles are 90° and 180°.

Two students discuss the molecular geometry of water (H_2O).

Student 1

Predicting the shape of a molecule is relatively straightforward. A molecule's shape will always be determined by the number of electron pairs around the central atom. The number of electron pairs corresponds to the number of atoms that are bound to the central atom of the molecule. For example, water contains two hydrogen atoms bound to one atom of oxygen, giving the molecule a linear geometry.

Student 2

The geometry of a molecule is dependent on the number of atoms bound to the central atom of that molecule. However, the geometry of a molecule is also dependent on the presence of electron pairs around the central atom that are not bonded to any atoms. These nonbonded electron pairs also have a negative charge and therefore repel the electrons that are bound to atoms, influencing the shape of a molecule. Because one molecule of water contains two nonbonded electron pairs around a central oxygen atom and two electron pairs bonded to hydrogen atoms, it has a tetrahedral geometry.

1. According to the passage, electron pairs tend to:

    A. attract each other.

    B. prefer a linear geometry.

    C. arrange themselves close to each other.

    D. arrange themselves as far apart as possible.

2. Based on Student 2's explanation, the south (negatively charged) end of a magnet will repel the south end of another magnet because:

    F. positive charges always attract each other.

    G. negative charges always repel each other.

    H. a positive and negative charge always attract each other.

    J. a positive and a negative charge always repel each other.

3. Suppose a molecule of sulfur dioxide (SO_2) was found to have a bond angle of 120° and contain one nonbonded electron pair. If true, this finding would most likely support the viewpoint(s) of:

    A. Student 1 only.

    B. Student 2 only.

    C. both Student 1 and Student 2.

    D. neither Student 1 nor Student 2.

4. Quantum mechanical models suggest that a molecule of sulfur hexafluoride (SF_6) contains no nonbonded electron pairs. Both students would predict that a molecule of SF_6 would have:

    F. an octahedral geometry.

    G. a trigonal bipyramidal geometry.

    H. bond angles of 90°, 120°, and 180°.

    J. a bond angle of 109.5°.

5. Suppose that the model presented by Student 1 is correct. Based on the information provided, what would be the bond angle in a molecule of percholrate ion (ClO_4^-)?

    A. 180°

    B. 120°

    C. 109.5°

    D. 90°

6. Based on the model presented by Student 1, a molecule of ammonia (NH_3) would have a:

   F. trigonal planar geometry, because three atoms of H are bound to one central atom of N.

   G. trigonal planar geometry, because three atoms of H and one unbound electron pair are bound to one central atom of N.

   H. tetrahedral geometry, because three atoms of H are bound to one central atom of N.

   J. tetrahedral geometry, because three atoms of H and one unbound electron pair are bound to one central atom of N.

7. Which of the following diagrams showing the relationship between an electron pair's bonded status and the relative strength of the repulsive force is consistent with Student 2's assertions about the shape of a water molecule, but is NOT consistent with Student 1's assertions about the shape of a water molecule?

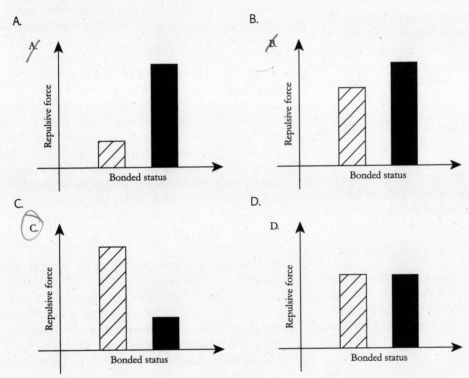

A.

B.

C.

D.

8. Measurements made through X-ray crystallography show that the repulsive force of non-bonded electron pairs is greater than the repulsive force of bound electron pairs. Based on the information provided, this finding would most likely weaken the viewpoint(s) of:

   F. Student 1 only.

   G. Student 2 only.

   H. both Student 1 and Student 2.

   J. neither Student 1 nor Student 2.

KAPLAN

ANSWERS AND EXPLANATIONS

1.   D

Remember that Conflicting Viewpoints passages can look a lot like Reading Comprehension passages. Here's a question that exemplifies that point; it tests our ability to locate and comprehend information from within the passage (information that just happens to be scientific, of course!). This is also a great question to answer first, because it doesn't require you to read either viewpoint yet.

To answer, we need to scan back through the opening information in the passage to find where it discusses electron pairs. That's in the second half of the second paragraph, which reads "VSEPR theory states that the shape of a molecule is determined by the repulsions between the bonded and nonbonded pairs of electrons in the outer shell of the molecule's central atom. These electron pairs arrange themselves as far apart as possible to minimize repulsion."

The last sentence perfectly matches choice (D), which is correct.

Notice that choices (A) and (C) get it exactly backward. This is a common wrong answer format. Choice (B) brings up a detail from later in the passage and uses it inappropriately, another common wrong answer format.

2.   G

To answer this question, we must apply what we know about charge from Student 2's explanation to a new situation (namely, magnets). What does Student 2 believe about negative charges? We should go back to the passage to find out.

Student 2 states that "nonbonded electron pairs also have a negative charge and therefore repel the electrons that are bound to atoms." This means that both bound and nonbound electron pairs have a negative charge, and that the two repel. We can conclude that negative charges repel each other.

Based on this theory, the south (negatively charged) end of a magnet will repel the negatively charged end of another magnet because negative charges always repel each other. This matches choice (G).

3.   B

This is a great example of the kind of question that can seem pretty complicated at first glance. It introduces a new type of molecule, gives us a bond angle, and asks us to figure out whose viewpoint is supported. But like most other Science questions, it breaks down to a series of relatively simple steps when we approach it methodically.

The chemical formula of sulfur dioxide is given to us in the question stem (SO_2). This is important because Student 1 states that you can determine the shape of a molecule from the chemical formula alone. All you have to do is count the "number of atoms that are bound to the central atom of a molecule." So we know that Student 1 would predict that a molecule of SO_2 would look just like a molecule of H_2O and according to him, a molecule of H_2O has a linear geometry. Unfortunately, the question stem doesn't give us the geometry of sulfur dioxide, just the bond angle, so we have a little more work to do.

To find the bond angle in a molecule with linear geometry, we need to consult the opening information again. That defines a linear molecule as having a bond angle of 180°. So, to put it all together, we know that Student 1 would believe that sulfur dioxide has a linear geometry and a bond angle of 180°. If it really has a bond angle of 120°, that does NOT support Student 1's viewpoint. So, we know the answer isn't choice (A) or (C).

Now we need to determine whether the fact that sulfur dioxide has a bond angle of 120° supports the viewpoint of Student 2. He states that "the geometry of a molecule is also dependent on the presence of electron pairs around the central atom that are not bonded to any atoms," and that because water contains two nonbonded pairs of electrons and two atoms bonded to the central atom, it has a tetrahedral geometry.

If a molecule of sulfur dioxide contains one nonbonded electron pair and two bound electron pairs, Student 2 would predict that it would have a trigonal planar geometry. According to the passage, this geometry has a bond angle of 120°. This is consistent with Student 2's viewpoint, so choice (B) is correct.

4. F

This question is asking us to make another prediction about molecular shape. This time, however, we're dealing with a situation in which Student 1 and Student 2 are in agreement. That's because according to the question stem, sulfur hexafluoride (SF_6) doesn't contain any nonbonded electron pairs, and these nonbonded electron pairs are the source of the two students' disagreement.

The question, then, is pretty straightforward. We have a central atom (S) with six atoms (F) bound to it. According to the information in the passage, molecules that contain six electron pairs around a central atom will have an octahedral geometry. Choice (F) is correct.

5. C

It would be wise to answer this question before reading Student 2's viewpoint, to minimize confusion.

Student 1 believes that "a molecule's shape will always be determined by the number of electron pairs around the central atom," and that "the number of electron pairs corresponds to the number of atoms that are bound to the central atom of the molecule." Because a molecule of percholrate ion (ClO_4^-) contains four O atoms around one central Cl atom, it should have a tetrahedral geometry.

The names of the possible shapes aren't given in the answer choices, just bond angles. According to the information in the passage, molecules with a tetrahedral geometry have bond angles of $109.5°$, and choice (C) is correct.

6. F

Here's another question we should answer before going on to read Student 2's viewpoint. Student 1 believes that the number of atoms bound to the central atom of a molecule determines the number of electron pairs around the central atom, and thus the shape of the molecule. If ammonia (NH_3) contains three H molecules around one N molecule, it should have a trigonal planar geometry. Choice (F) is correct.

If we look at the remaining answer choices, we can see that the wrong choices are drawn from either Student 2's viewpoint alone, or a combination of Student 1 and Student 2's viewpoints. Answering this question before we go on to read Student 2's viewpoint will help us avoid a lot of potential confusion.

7. D

The first step in answering this question is to make sure we know exactly what Student 1 and Student 2 assert about the strength of the repulsive force of bonded and nonbonded electron pairs.

Student 1 claims that nonbonded electron pairs don't factor into the shape of a molecule at all. That's why water has a linear geometry, he says. Student 2 claims that nonbonded electron pairs exert a repulsive force equal in magnitude to the repulsive force exerted by bonded electron pairs. That's why he believes a molecule of water, which contains two bonded and two nonbonded electron pairs, should have a tetrahedral geometry.

So, we're looking for a diagram that shows the relative strength of the repulsive force to be equal for bonded and nonbonded electron pairs. This is consistent with choice (D), which shows the two bars to be of equal length. Choice (D), then, is correct.

Note that the question stem asks us to determine which answer choice is consistent with Student 2's viewpoint and not Student 1's. It doesn't matter what we might know about the repulsive force of bonded and nonbonded electrons, or which student is actually right in this case (if either). Our job is simply to identify the diagram that is consistent with the viewpoints in the passage.

8. H

According to the passage, Student 1 believes that nonbonded electron pairs don't factor into the shape of a molecule. Measurements that prove nonbonded electron pairs *do* show a repulsive force would weaken his viewpoint, because this would allow them to influence the shape of the molecule. We can eliminate choices (G) and (J).

We're not done, though. We still need to determine whether this information weakens the viewpoint of Student 2. He believes that nonbonded electron pairs behave just like bonded electron pairs in determining the shape of a molecule. If measurements were to show that nonbonded electron pairs exerted a repulsive force *greater* than that of bound electron pairs, his viewpoint would also be weakened—nonbonded electron pairs could not be counted on to behave just like bound electron pairs, and would have an even greater influence on the shape of a molecule than he believes. His viewpoint would also be weakened, so choice (H) is correct.

KAPLAN

Chapter Twenty: **Conflicting Viewpoints III**

COMPLEX PASSAGES

Some passages are just more complex than others. Some seem complex to one person but not another because the subject matter isn't his or her favorite science topic. While you're more likely to see some simpler (for you) and more complex (for you) topics among the Data Representation or Research Summaries passages simply because there are three each of those, you might get a Conflicting Viewpoints passage that seems really complex, or just isn't your cup of tea. That's OK; don't let it psych you out. There are ways of dealing with complex Conflicting Viewpoints passages, and we're going to finish up the Conflicting Viewpoints section by looking at them.

If you come across a Conflicting Viewpoints passage that immediately strikes you as really confusing, relax, take a deep breath, and remember that you're prepared for this test and you're going to do well (it's the power of positive thinking, and it really works). Then, start reading attentively; nothing gets your mind wandering like a topic that just doesn't interest you. The passages are short, though, so stay focused. Be on the lookout for the authors' main points—they usually sum up their beliefs in one neat thesis sentence. Underline it when you see it. If you finish reading a viewpoint without finding a thesis sentence, check the first and last paragraphs of the viewpoint again. They're most often there, but unfortunately not always. If you don't see a thesis statement, don't worry. Move on to the questions and refer back to individual details of the viewpoint as necessary.

When you finish reading one viewpoint, skip ahead to the questions and answer the ones that relate to just that viewpoint. This will give you the chance to solidify your understanding of that viewpoint before reading any others. It'll also break up the passage into even smaller chunks, making it less likely that you'll zone out and waste time reading without comprehending. With only eight questions in the passage, though, not every viewpoint will have questions about just it. If you do get some, take advantage!

Sometimes, especially if the opening information is rather long, you'll get a question or two that relates to just that. It's worth it to check the questions for ones that relate to just the opening info (look for ones that start with a vague, "According to the passage…").

When you're done answering any questions that relate to only the first viewpoint, go ahead and read the second, and answer the questions that relate to just that viewpoint (repeat this process if there are more than two viewpoints). Finally, you can answer the questions that relate to

KAPLAN)

multiple viewpoints. Remember that you can answer questions in any order you'd like, so skip the really difficult-looking ones on the first pass.

COMPLEX QUESTIONS

Questions can also get complex. Most often, the ACT makes a question complex by veering pretty far from what is directly stated in the passage. They might do this by introducing seemingly unrelated concepts, asking you to make a prediction or draw a conclusion that feels pretty abstract, or asking you to apply a scientist's reasoning to an entirely new situation.

Complex questions ARE answerable. Start by making sure you understand exactly what the author is saying. Reread the relevant parts of the passage and summarize the main idea in your own words (to yourself, of course!). Then, go straight to the answer choices. Three will contain fatal flaws. Look for these. The most common kind of wrong answer choice uses ideas drawn from the wrong parts of the passage (for example, ideas in the opening information or another author's viewpoint). Also look out for answer choices that use just the right words but actually state the exact opposite of what is true, answer choices that use key words from the passage but aren't relevant to the question at hand (these are always tempting because they *look* so good), and answer choices that are outside of the scope of the passage. An answer choice doesn't have to be one you'd come up with on your own to be correct—it just has to be true according to the passage.

Finally, remember that you do have a time limit. Don't spend too much time on any one question. Guess, circle it in your test booklet, and come back for another look if you have time when you finish the section.

PRACTICE QUESTIONS

PASSAGE III

Scientists discuss three possible explanations for the mechanism by which water (H_2O) conducts electric current.

Scientist 1

Pure water is incapable of conducting an electric current. Electric current in this sense is defined as the flow of electrically charged particles, known as electrons, through a medium. Because the electrons in a water molecule are tightly bound to the molecule, they will not flow freely and cannot create an electric current.

Pure water will, however, conduct ions—that is, charged particles within the water will physically move from one place to another when an electric charge is applied. However, the physical flow of ions from one location to another is technically different from the flow of electric current, so it cannot be accurately stated that water conducts electric current.

Scientist 2

Water itself is capable of conducting electricity, but it does so very poorly. The hydrogen and oxygen in water molecules continuously **dissociate** (come apart) into H^+ and OH^- ions and reform into H_2O. As the bonds in water are continuously broken and reformed, electrons are temporarily freed. When an electric field or current is then applied to water, the electrons that constitute the electric current are able to flow from one end to another, constituting a feeble electric current. The individual H^+ and OH^- ions are not required to move in this process, so the result is the flow of a true electric current.

When a substance that suppresses the formation of ions is dissolved in water, it will no longer conduct electricity. So when sugar, for example, is stirred into water, the production of ions is disrupted, and the water will cease to conduct electricity. When a substance that increases ion concentration is added to water, the water will conduct a greater amount of electricity.

Scientist 3

Water is capable of conducting electricity, but only because it contains impurities. Most water contains dissolved salts, such as sodium chloride (NaCl), minerals, such as calcium (Ca) and copper (Cu), and gasses, such as carbon dioxide (CO_2). The impurities dissolved in water are capable of conducting an electric current because they contain unpaired electrons in the atoms' outer valence shells. It is these unpaired valence electrons that permit the flow of electric current. The number of electrons available to transmit charge is proportional to the amount of electricity the water can conduct.

Seawater is a perfect example of how impurities are responsible for the electrical conductivity of water. Seawater primarily contains dissolved sodium (Na^+), chloride (Cl^-), sulfate (SO_4^{2-}), magnesium (Mg^{2+}), calcium (Ca^{2+}), and potassium (K^+) ions. While pure water can conduct approximately 0.000055 $S \cdot m^{-1}$ (Siemens per meter) of electricity, seawater can conduct 5 $S \cdot m^{-1}$. The concentration of dissolved impurities is also directly proportional to the conductivity of water; the saltier the water, the more electricity it can conduct.

1. Based on Scientist 3's explanation, if the number of unpaired electrons in the valence shells of the impurities in water were decreased, which of the following quantities would simultaneously decrease?

    A. The resistivity of water.

    B. The electrical conductivity of the water.

    C. The H^+ concentration of the water.

    D. The density of the water.

2. Which scientist(s), if any, would predict that water will not truly conduct an electric current if it is 100% pure?

    F. Scientist 1, but not Scientist 2 or Scientist 3.

    G. Scientist 2, but not Scientist 1 or Scientist 3.

    H. Both Scientist 1 and Scientist 2, but not Scientist 3.

    J. Both Scientist 1 and Scientist 3, but not Scientist 2.

3. City A's drinking water is typically heavily chlorinated, resulting in the formation of hypochlorite ions (ClO^-). Scientist 3 would most likely predict that, compared to less-chlorinated water, City A's water would show:

    A. an increase in the amount of electricity the water is capable of conducting.

    B. a decrease in the amount of electricity the water is capable of conducting.

    C. no change in the amount of electricity the water is capable of conducting.

    D. a decrease in the formation of H^+ ions.

4. When a sample of zinc (Zn) is doped with chromium (Cr), the electrical conductivity at room temperature is increased fivefold. Based on Scientist 3's explanation, the reason that the conductivity increases is most likely that:

    F. the addition of Cr allows for the formation of ions within the sample.

    G. Cr atoms contain fewer electrons in their outer valence shells than Zn atoms.

    H. Cr atoms contain more electrons in their outer valence shells than Zn atoms.

    J. Cr is a better conductor of electricity because it is a metal.

5. Salt (NaCl) in water ionizes to form Na$^+$ and Cl$^-$ ions. When an electric current is passed through a dish of pure water mixed with salt, a current is conducted. Scientist 1 would most likely argue that:

   A. an ion flow, not a true electric current, has been conducted.

   B. a true electric current, not an ion flow, has been conducted.

   C. the salt encourages H$^+$ and OH$^-$ ions to form, resulting in an electric current.

   D. the salt disrupts H$^+$ and OH$^-$ ion formation, reducing the maximum possible electric current.

6. Suppose it is found that the more water is heated, the more readily it dissociates into H$^+$ and OH$^-$ ions. Scientist 2 would most likely state that a greater electric current could be conducted by:

   F. cooler water than by warmer water.

   G. warmer water than by cooler water.

   H. ice than liquid water.

   J. a mixture of ice and water than by liquid water.

7. Both Scientist 2 and Scientist 3 would most likely agree that water will conduct more electricity under which of the following conditions?

   A. The water is purified of any impurities.

   B. The water is polarized.

   C. Sugar is added to the water.

   D. Ion-producing impurities are added to the water.

8. Suppose it is discovered that in the presence of an electric current, water readily ionizes into H$^+$ and OH$^-$ ions. This finding would support the viewpoint of:

   F. both Scientist 1 and Scientist 2.

   G. both Scientist 1 and Scientist 3.

   H. Scientist 2 only.

   J. neither Scientist 1, nor Scientist 2, nor Scientist 3.

ANSWERS AND EXPLANATIONS

1. B

To answer this question, we must make sure we understand what Scientist 3 has to say about unpaired electrons in the valence shells of impurities in water. In his first paragraph, she states, "The impurities dissolved in water are capable of conducting an electric current because they contain unpaired electrons in the atoms' outer valence shells. It is these unpaired valence electrons that permit the flow of electric current. The number of electrons available to transmit charge is proportional to the amount of electricity the water can conduct."

This is complicated, so it is crucial that we make sure we really understand his point. Scientist 3 is saying that unpaired electrons in the outer shells of impurities in water conduct electricity. Furthermore, she's saying that the more electrons you have available, the more electricity you can conduct.

If more valence electrons mean more electricity can be conducted, then what would happen if there were fewer valence electrons? A smaller electric current could be conducted. That is, if the number of available electrons decreased, the electrical conductivity of the water would decrease. Choice (B) is correct.

2. J

This question is asking us to predict what each scientist would believe about the ability of pure water to truly conduct electricity. Let's work methodically, starting with Scientist 1.

Scientist 1 states in the first sentence that "Pure water is incapable of conducting an electric current." He does, however, concede that pure water is capable of conducting ions. He clarifies at the end, though, that "the physical flow of ions from one location to another is technically different from the flow of electric current, so it cannot be accurately stated that water conducts electric current." Scientist 1 agrees that water will not truly conduct an electric current if it is 100% pure, so we can eliminate choice (G).

Scientist 2 believes that pure water is capable of conducting electricity: "Water itself is capable of conducting electricity, but it does so very poorly." He also states that the flow is "a true electric current." Since Scientist 2 disagrees with the statement in the question stem, we can eliminate choice (H).

Scientist 3 believes that water is capable of conducting electricity, but "only because it contains impurities." Pure water, then, would not conduct electricity in his opinion. He agrees with the statement in the question stem, so choice (J) is correct.

3. A

We have to make sure we understand Scientist 3's viewpoint before we attempt to answer this question. He writes that "the impurities dissolved in water are capable of conducting an electric current because they contain unpaired electrons in the atoms' outer valence shells," and that "the number of electrons available to transmit charge is proportional to the amount of electricity the water can conduct." He also ends his discussion of why seawater conducts electricity by noting that "the concentration of dissolved impurities is also directly proportional to the conductivity of water."

It makes sense, then, that Scientist 3 would believe that City A's water, with its greater concentration of hypochlorite ions, would conduct more electricity than less heavily chlorinated water. Choice (A) is correct.

Note that choice (B) gets the relationship backward, and choice (D) introduces a detail from Scientist 2's argument. Both of these answer choices might be tempting if we didn't take the time to review Scientist 3's viewpoint.

4. H

Again, we need to start answering this question by making sure we understand Scientist 3's viewpoint. He writes that "unpaired valence electrons…permit the flow of electric current. The number of electrons available to transmit charge is proportional to the amount of electricity the water can conduct."

Basically, this means that electric current flows in water because of the availability of valence electrons. The more electrons you have, the more electricity you can conduct.

Now, we need to apply this same line of reasoning to the example in the question stem. When chromium is added to a sample of zinc, the sample can conduct five times more electricity. According to Scientist 3's line of reasoning, this must be because chromium has more valence electrons free to transmit charge. This matches choice (H).

Choice (F) is incorrect. Scientist 2 is the one talking about ions.

Choice (G) is incorrect because it states the exact opposite of what is true.

Choice (J) is incorrect because it is unrelated to the passage.

5. A

This is a great question to answer first, before reading Scientist 2 or Scientist 3's viewpoints.

Scientist 1 states that "pure water will…conduct ions—that is, charged particles within the water will physically move from one place to another when an electric charge is applied. However, the physical flow of ions from one location to another is technically different from the flow of electric current, so it cannot be accurately stated that water conducts electric current."

The question stem tells us that salt forms ions in water. We should assume, then, that Scientist 1 would think that, while perhaps more current is conducted, it is still technically an ion flow, and not a true current. Choice (A) is correct.

Note that choice (B) states the exact opposite of what we'd expect Scientist 1 to say, and choices (C) and (D) are drawn from Scientist 2's viewpoint.

6. G

Here's a prime example of a question that seems confusing because it introduces some apparently unrelated information (water temperature wasn't discussed at all in the passage). But we'll take it one step at a time. First, let's review what Scientist 2 has to say about ions. He states that "the hydrogen and oxygen in water molecules continuously *dissociate* (come apart) into H^+ and OH^- ions and reform into H_2O. As the bonds in water are continuously broken and reformed, electrons are temporarily freed.

When an electric field or current is then applied to water, the electrons that constitute the electric current are able to flow from one end to another, constituting a feeble electric current." The result, he says, is "the flow of a true electric current."

The question stem tells us that the more water is heated, the more H^+ and OH^- ions it forms. We can put these two pieces of information together; warmer water has more ions and therefore must conduct more electricity. (According to Scientist 2 and the information in the question, anyway. Remember, it doesn't matter which viewpoint is true as long as you're using the one the question asks for!) Choice (G) is correct.

7. D

Another "which of the following" question. Our protocol here is to make sure we understand each viewpoint, then move directly to the answer choices.

Scientist 2 believes that the ions in water are responsible for conducting electricity. Since water essentially self-ionizes into H^+ and OH^- ions, it can conduct electricity even when no other ions are present.

Scientist 3 believes that only the presence of added ions, in the form of impurities, makes water able to conduct electricity. The two disagree over whether pure water can conduct electricity, but not over the fact that ions are essential for electricity conduction in water. Now the answer choices:

Choice (A) is incorrect. Scientist 3 specifically states that impurities are necessary for the conduction of an electric current.

Choice (B) is incorrect. No one ever mentions polarization. This is outside the scope of the passage.

Choice (C) is incorrect. Scientist 2 actually states that adding sugar to water will make it unable to conduct electricity. We're looking for something that will make water conduct *more* electricity.

Choice (D) is correct. Both scientists agree that ions are responsible for electricity conduction in water. More ions would therefore lead to more electricity conducted.

8. H

By now we can readily recognize that H^+ and OH^- ion formation is the key to Scientist 2's viewpoint. He believes that the ability of water to self-ionize into H^+ and OH^- ions is responsible for its ability to conduct electricity. If it was discovered that the application of an electric current made water ionize into H^+ and OH^- ions even more easily, his argument would be strengthened. Choice (H) is correct.

Getting Prepared for Medical School

Congratulations on acing the MCAT and getting accepted to medical school! Your hard work in your undergraduate courses and your dedication to studying have led to this great success.

The next step in your journey is four years of medical school, filled with new experiences every step of the way. Intensive coursework, your first exposure to real patients, and USMLE exams are just some of the challenges you will face. Don't let this unnerve you—you've got Kaplan Medical on your side to help you succeed every step of the way. Kaplan Medical offers the most realistic, complete, up-to-date, and effective medical school content review and USMLE prep through live lectures, video lectures, books, and online products.

Here are some tips from the Kaplan Medical staff that you may find useful in making an easier transition into the life of a first-year medical student.

Should I Join a Note-Taking Coop?

Note taking coops have pros and cons. They fill the gaps if you have to miss a lecture due to illness or an unexpected emergency, but they may be distributed long after the lecture, which means you'll have little time to study material that is presented just before exams.

Should I Buy Every Textbook Offered?

Before you buy textbooks, check with upperclassmen to see what they bought or regretted buying.

How Can I Study for My Classes and the USMLE?

USMLE review materials such as Kaplan's *MedEssentials* are great condensed versions of the most important principles and concepts that your faculty will expect you to master. Using review material now and personalizing it with your high lightings and marginalia means that they'll be familiar and super useful when you begin preparing for Step 1. Go to your favorite bookstore or **kaptest.com/store** to get your copy before you head back into the classroom.

Establish a Study Space.

Pick an area on campus or in your house that you visit *only* when it's time to buckle down and study for class or the USMLE. Used regularly for just this purpose, that space will actually help you focus and get down to business each time you visit it.

Preview for Upcoming Lecture Topics

USMLE review books can help create a mental framework so that you'll get more out of hearing your class lectures.

Prep Your Life So It Doesn't Get in the Way of School

Be sure to settle in before classes begin so the process won't intrude on needed study time. Here are some tasks that you should plan to complete before your first day of classes:

- Scout out grocery stores, ATMs, gas stations, laundry/dry cleaning stores convenient to your school and housing

- Establish banking, utilities, internet, or other services that you'll need

- Finalize housing arrangements and set up your living space

- Reach out to students ahead of you for advice

- Reach out to classmates to form study partners

- Begin building a support network

- Understand your school's curriculum design:

    - Traditional (by subject)

    - Organ System or Problem-based

    - Mix of both

Congratulations on your successes so far and good luck with medical school!

For more information on Kaplan Medical products and services go to kaplanmedical.com